As Re

Making I

"*Most people realize that living a good life is highly dependent on making good decisions. Stunningly, there has never been a method that teaches us how to do so! Humanity has been like a mariner out to sea without a sextant or a compass. In that context, this may be the most impactful book you'll ever read. Anyone willing to apply its simple genius can immediately begin making more powerful, life-enhancing choices.*"

- Steve D'Annunzio, *President of Mission Driven Advisors*

"*Brian Whetten's book cuts like a diamond through all the new age narcissistic glass ceilings posing as spirituality and delivers a tool for understanding and then trusting Intuition, the ultimate decision-maker.*"

- Steve Chandler, Best Selling Author of 30 books including *Time Warrior* and *100 Ways to Motivate Yourself*

"*Not only will you gain insight into the realm of intuition and choice-making, Brian Whetten demystifies the hidden process of effective decision making in this straight talking new book. It's indispensible.*"

- Barnet Bain, Producer of *What Dreams May Come*

"*Yes Yes Hell No! is an incredibly powerful book for anyone wanting to move forward in their life and in their business. It teaches a simple but extraordinary tool for making any big decision with ease!*"

- Kristi Joba, COO of CoachesWithClients.com

As Recommended for Business Leaders

"For anyone struggling with an inner call to be an agent of change or a transformative leader, this book will provide you with important insights on how to overcome those inner demons and shift from fear to forward movement."

- Dr. Andre Delbecq, Professor of Management at Santa Clara University

"Brian Whetten has created a simple, powerful tool for decision-making that gets into your bones, immediately affecting all of your decisions starting the day you read his book. Yes, Yes, Hell No is an essential guide to being an intuitive, effective, and innovative leader. Highly recommended."

- Brennan Smith, Author of *The Art of Inspired Action*

"Yes, Yes, Hell No! is a must read for decision makers. If you're a business leader or someone who supports business leaders, this remarkable, easy to read book delivers cutting edge wisdom on how to increase your ability to make great decisions, eliminate procrastination, and achieve your highest goals."

- Gary Henson, Founder, BusinessCoach.com

As Recommended for Finding and Living Your Life's Purpose

"As a cardiologist, I regularly meet with patients who have had a heart attack and are taking a hard look at their lives. 'Did I make the right choices? What is the purpose of my life? Did my life matter?' These are some of the most important questions, and this book contains one of the most powerful tools I've ever seen for finding your own answers, and creating a fulfilled life."

- Victor Kubbeh, MD

"Doing what you're here to do, and being who you're here to be, requires the powerful practice of consistently making decisions for your highest good. This book contains one of the most life changing tools for helping you do just that."

- Christine Kloser, Best Selling Author and Founder of the Transformational Author Experience

"I've used Brian's book with clients and found it invaluable in propelling their change forward. It has helped create deep shifts with clients and allowed our time together to be dramatically more powerful. Providing a copy to clients is a gift to the coaching relationship, taking it to the next level."

- Ella McQuinn, Executive Coach and Leadership Consultant

As Recommended for Coaches, Counselors, Healers and Helping Professionals

"Yes, Yes, Hell No is a brilliant road map for achieving success and fulfillment in life and business that draws from the wisdom of the ages as well as today's most leading edge research on spirituality and personal growth. I love, love, love the simplicity and truth to the 'Yes, Yes, Hell No' model of making life's most important decisions. Highly recommended reading for counselors, coaches, therapists and any helping professionals whose clients struggle with their choices, but this plainly and clearly written book is best suited for anyone who wants to tap into their inner compass and live their best life with meaning, purpose, personal success, financial freedom, and fulfillment."

- David Steele, MA, LMFT, CLC; Founder, Relationship Coaching Institute

"Coaches help people change their lives for the better. But there is a paradox – the more important and heartfelt a goal is, the scarier it can be to pursue it. Yes Yes Hell No! shows exactly why this is so, and provides simple and powerful tools for resolving these paradoxes, and to help coaches enroll clients effectively. I highly recommend it."

- Joseph O'Connor, Best Selling Author of *Introducing NLP*, Founder of the International Coaching Community

As Recommended for Creating
the Life of Your Dreams

"This book nails the issue of why so many people fail to move forward on the dreams they claim to want so badly, yet are scared to commit to. It provides a simple, proven, transformational tool for how to take action on your desires, find your purpose, and fulfill your dreams. A masterful package of wisdom!"

- John Renesch, Author, *The Great Growing Up*; Co-founder, FutureShapers

"I have to say 'bravo!' Reading Yes, Yes, Hell No! is one of the most eye-opening things you can do. The principles of this book, when applied, can lead anyone from where they are to whatever level of growth and development they want to achieve."

- Bill Baren, CEO of Bill Baren Coaching

YES YES HELL NO!
The Little Book for Making Big Decisions

Published by: Spiritual Roar Publications
www.spiritualroar.com
ISBN: 978-0-9-863090-0-7

Printed in the United States of America

A portion of the proceeds from the sale of this book will be donated to the charities the author supports.

YES
YES
HELL NO!

THE LITTLE BOOK FOR MAKING
BIG DECISIONS

BRIAN WHETTEN, PH.D.
Foreword by JACK CANFIELD

To the love of my life.

*Thank you for trusting my love even when I was
blinded by fear.*

Foreword

by Jack Canfield
Co-author of *The Success Principles*™ and Co-creator of the
Chicken Soup for the Soul® series

When I was born in 1944, virtually the entire world was at war. Seventy years later, a potent mix of technology and democracy has transformed our planet, and created an unprecedented level of financial prosperity.

Yet many people are still deeply unhappy.

Not because they have so few opportunities in life, but because they have so many.

Once upon a time, life was simple. You went to school, got a job, followed the rules, and did your best to raise a family. There were lots of difficulties, but not as many expectations. There were many more dangers to deal with, but not as many decisions to make.

In the twenty-first century, life has become defined by two things: *choice* and *change*. Yet few people have been trained in how to make great choices and effectively deal with change.

Consider just making the choice of what product to buy. As of today, Amazon lists over 227 million choices. How do you choose whom to marry? There were 17 million people last month on Match.com alone. How do you choose what job you want to take? At any given time, Monster.com lists over a million open positions.

Or perhaps you'd like to find a new religion? Type "join a religion" into Google and you'll receive 230,000,000 results. Interested in self-help? There are 1.7 *billion* links to choose from.

Given all these different choices, it's getting harder and harder to trust that you've made the best ones. This is stressful, and it creates a lot of second-guessing, self-judgment and regret.

Now, this might not be so bad, except for the fact that the world is changing, faster and faster with each and every day. And while we may be free to choose, more and more we are required to change.

Everything in nature is either growing or dying. Always. And the faster our world keeps changing, the more important it is that we do, too.

Recent research shows that 65 percent of current preschool students will work in a type of job that doesn't even exist yet. Every 2 days, we now create as much information as was generated from the dawn of mankind through 2003. For someone working on a technical degree, more than half the information they learn in their first year will be out of date by the time they graduate.

The information age has turned into the information *overload* age. Technology, for all its good, has created a transformational tread wheel, where it feels like we have to run ever faster just to keep up.

This has become the defining challenge in business, in leadership and in life. It's no longer enough just to work hard and do what you're told. Lasting success and happiness now requires mastering two critical skills – the ability to choose and the ability to change. It requires learning how to make the right big decisions and how to create big wins in an ever more challenging world.

Thankfully, over the past seventy years, we've developed an equally remarkable set of transformational technologies for helping people do just that. As one example, the 64 principles I lay out in my book *The Success Principles*™ aren't just a set of good ideas. They're a proven, powerful technology for growing, changing, and improving your life in remarkable ways.

Yet while many people know about all these new transformational technologies, far fewer have invested the time and energy to truly master them and put them to use.

The reason for this is that while much of this field has been described as "self-help," true transformation requires asking for support – over and over again. And for most of us this is scary.

It's scary to admit you have a problem. It's scary to ask for help, and it's scary to open yourself up to receiving support. It's scary to commit to your most heartfelt goals, because it's scary to risk failing. And as strange as it might sound, it's also scary to risk succeeding.

The paradox of growth is that the more you care about a goal – such as getting married, having a child, finding your calling, transforming your company's culture, or waking up to who you really are – the more that a piece of you will say "Yes Yes" to that goal, another piece of you will say "Hell No!"

As you'll discover from reading this book, when you experience this *Yes Yes Hell No!* the answer is to go forward and get support in doing so. Yet this is the opposite of what most people do. Instead of creating a big win, or making a big decision, we put things off. We procrastinate. We numb out. We look for something that feels safe and nonthreatening. We avoid choosing. We put off changing. But in doing so, we experience ever more stress, anxiety and frustration. And we mortgage the exciting and fulfilling life we could be living for a false sense of security.

Does this resonate for you? Would you like to master the ability to make great decisions and create powerful, positive changes in your life? And would you like to release the fears that come up as you do so?

If so, do not put this book down. Do not pass go. Do not collect $200. Read this book. Do the exercises and apply what you learn. This book is short and easy to read, yet the simple tools it contains are extremely powerful and will change your life.

You are about to discover one of the most simple and powerful technologies I've ever seen for making big decisions in life and for creating the big wins you want and deserve. You are also going to learn a new and radically powerful process for transforming your fears. You are going to have the opportunity to get clear on what it is you most want in life, and you're going to receive sure-fire guidance in how to go and get it.

In the midst of an ever more rapidly changing world, you're now going to learn a powerful tool you can trust, from one of the great leaders and coaches in the field.

Contents

Section II: How Your Life Improves With Each Yes Yes Hell No!

Section III:

Learning to Recognize the Many Faces of Fear

Section IV: Ten Steps to Mastery

Introduction

W hat does it take to create an extraordinary life? One where you make a difference, have amazing relationships, achieve your dreams, live your purpose, and experience great happiness?

You have to be able to:

- **Make big decisions.** A big decision is a choice where the stakes are high and you feel conflicted about the alternatives.

- **Create big wins.** A big win is a goal that's heartfelt, specific, and scary. It's a dream or a desire that matters so much it frightens you.

- **Make friends with your fears.** The problem with big wins and big decisions is that they trigger your fears. And the harder you fight against those fears, the stronger they become. Instead, your opportunity is to release the inner conflict by learning how to turn your fears into some of your most trustworthy friends.

This book contains what may be the single most powerful and reliable tool there is for developing these three skills. This tool works in a wide range of areas. It's free, fun, and non-fattening. Plus it creates remarkable results.

This book will teach you how.

In it, you're going to discover how to find and take action on a *Yes Yes Hell No!* This simple process may be the single most powerful and effective tool there is for creating big wins, making big decisions, and turning your fears into an ally and friend.

When used properly, this tool is guaranteed to help you create inspiring goals and make great decisions in any area of your life. It's as close to 100 percent accurate as any process or practice that I've ever seen. It's been the secret to my successes and to the successes of my clients.

This tool works in business and leadership. It works in families and relationship. It works in religion and spirituality. And it works in your daily life.

If you learn how to use this tool and then practice it consistently, it will change your life in profound ways.

As you read this book, you'll notice the occasional use of words like "spirit," "soul," "faith," and "purpose." Please don't take this to mean that you're reading a religious book. While the tool you're about to learn is compatible with all the great religions, it doesn't require any particular set of religious beliefs.

You can use this tool if you consider yourself to be religious, atheist, agnostic, spiritual, pagan, a Cubs fan, or just about anything else.

This book doesn't deal with theology or morality. Instead, it's the result of repeatedly asking a single question.

"What works?"

The purpose of this book is not to convince you of any particular viewpoint. It's to help you take more effective actions toward more consciously chosen choices.

My goal is to provide you with a life-changing, practical tool for helping you get more of everything you most want in life.

I know. It's a big intention and some big claims.

Please. Read the book. See if it resonates with you. If so, try the tool out. Discover if it works for you. If it does, please take it as a gift. Keep it, use it, and make it your own. Share it with others.

And if it doesn't work for any reason, that's fine too. Please keep trying other tools until you find ones that work for you.

There are four sections to this book, each comprised of a series of short, small chapters. The first section explains *what* the tool is and what it means to experience a *Yes Yes Hell No!* The second section explains *why* this tool works so well, and why it produces such profound, consistent, life changing results. The third section explores *the essential skill* for using this tool – the ability to identify the many different faces of fear. And the final section shares *how* to use this tool in a set of simple, easy to learn steps.

Now, I know you might be tempted to jump right to the back of the book and to read through the tool itself. But please, slow down. Take things one section at a time. This little book covers a lot of ground.

In it you're going to learn how to create more of everything you most want in life. How to release the fears that have been holding you back. How to reliably harness the power of intuition. The keys to creating amazing relationships. How to find your purpose. The practical power of faith. And even the meaning of life.

While this book contains a great deal of valuable *information*, its greatest power is as a technology for *transformation*. Each chapter in this book includes one or more questions and exercises, which are contained in a separate, complimentary workbook. To get the most value from this book, please visit *www.YesYesHellNo.com*, download and print this companion guide, and use it as you first discover and then master this life changing tool.

Note: Some of the stories in this book have been changed to protect client confidentiality. The essence of their experiences remains intact, while their names and identifying details have been altered.

Section I

DISCOVERING THE POWER OF A YES YES HELL NO!

One Choice Can Change Your Life Forever

"Tell me, what is it you plan to do with your one wild and precious life?" ~ Mary Oliver

B eing cold and drunk is probably not the best tool for making big decisions. Yet one time, it really worked for me.

I made this particular choice on a cold winter night as I was stumbling home from the bars. After nineteen years of living in a small, safe, Midwestern college town, it was time to decide which graduate schools to apply to. The deadline was just around the corner, and I needed to make a big decision. Did I want to stay with what was familiar – a great engineering school in the middle of a very large cornfield? Or did I want to try something new? And if so, which of the many possible schools did I want to apply to?

The choices were daunting.

After weeks of procrastination, it took a blizzard for me to make up my mind. I don't know if it was the alcohol warming my blood or the ice-cold wind freezing my face, but in that moment I suddenly got it: I'd had enough of winter. Permanently. In a fit of defiance, I screamed at the snow "I will never be this cold again!"

And I meant it.

The next day, I ripped up the applications for all the schools that weren't in California. I applied to my two top picks. And I waited.

Stanford turned me down.

Berkeley let me in.

Thank God.

So I moved to California and wore shorts every day for a year. As a matter of principle.

That one little decision changed my life forever. It introduced me to a whole new world of opportunities and put me on a radically different path.

Living in the International House and making friends from dozens of countries. Raising $20 million for two Silicon Valley startups as my first job out of college. Making and losing millions, three times, before I turned thirty. Having millionaires as roommates because they wanted someone to help with their dogs. Working 90 hours a week, every week, for four years in a row. Burning out twice, because once wasn't enough. Getting a master's degree in Spiritual Psychology, because what else could follow a Ph.D. in Computer Science? Reinventing my career – again. Meeting the love of my life, getting married, and having our two amazing daughters.

None of it would have happened if it wasn't for that one crucial choice.

Twenty years later, I feel like I'm living a charmed life. It certainly isn't safe or predictable, and it certainly hasn't been free from pain, loss and failure.

Yet, my life has also become better than I could have imagined.

Not because there's something special about me, but because there's something special about the way I've learned to make decisions.

Without knowing it, I stumbled on a remarkable tool early in my life. It's the surest technology I know of for making great choices. When practiced consistently, this tool creates total trust in your ability to create big wins and make big decisions. It allows you to release your fears and insecurities. And it leads to getting more of everything you most want.

My life is a testament to this tool. It's a process that's simple, practical, and accurate. It applies to a wide range of situations. Used correctly, it's virtually infallible. And it's familiar. You've probably already used it in your life without knowing it. I had. Over and over and over again. I even used it on that cold, dark, drunken night, all those years ago.

I just didn't know it at the time.

It took me many years to discover what this tool is and why it works.

With this book, you can learn it in a matter of hours.

Would that be valuable?

If so, welcome. Please hold on tight and enjoy the ride.

Chapter 2

Big Wins and Big Decisions

"If you always make the right decision, the safe decision, the one most people make, you will be the same as everyone else." ~ Paul Arden

How do you make decisions? Do you know? It may be the single most important choice you make. It's the master decision which determines all the others.

Expert decision makers lead extraordinary lives. They create remarkable results. They become exceptional leaders. They have an outsized impact in the world. They make the most of each day. And they receive tremendous rewards.

Yet few of us are ever taught how to make great decisions.

Think about it. How do you make your decisions? Do you weigh the pros and cons? Listen to your gut? Flip a coin? Phone a friend?

Do you throw yourself into a grinding process of trial and error? Or do you hang back, hoping that someone else will make your decisions for you?

If you're reading this book, you've almost certainly learned how to make *good* decisions. Heck, you're alive, breathing and reading – and that says something.

But great decisions? Where was the college course on that? Where exactly were we supposed to learn this all important skill?

In the United States, between 40-50 percent of all first marriages and 60 percent of second marriages will end in divorce. The U.S. Department of Labor estimates that today's graduates will have ten to fourteen jobs by the age of thirty-eight. And even if you make it to the top, the average tenure of a Fortune 500 CEO is now only 4.6 years. Research by Gallup shows that 70 percent of full-time employees either hate their work or have disengaged from it to the point that they're costing their companies money. And according to a recent Harris poll, only 33 percent of Americans describe themselves as being very happy.

One of the biggest problems today is that in order to be successful we have to make ever more decisions in the face of ever faster changes, without being taught how to effectively do so. Growing up, we're taught biology instead of emotional intelligence. We're taught about how life started instead of how to effectively live it.

This book addresses that problem.

Imagine. How would your life change if you had complete trust in your ability to make great decisions? What challenges might you take on? What mistakes could you avoid? What successes would you achieve?

That's what we're going to help you start to create.

In order to create an extraordinary life, there are two types of decisions you need to master: *dilemmas* and *dreams*. Of the two, dilemmas are the more common. These are where you have to choose between two or more alternatives, such as whether you want to get married to someone you're in a relationship with or end it, or whether you want to stay with a safe but unfulfilling job or take a risk on a new, more meaningful career. A dilemma can feel like a choice between two bad outcomes, but it doesn't have to be. What matters is that the decision is important to you and that you feel conflicted over making a decision.

A *Big Decision* is a dilemma where the stakes are high and you feel emotionally conflicted about your choices.

These are the forks in the road where your choice matters, and you feel torn between the alternatives. These decisions can be large, such as choosing which college to go to, or small, such as choosing how you react when someone you love upsets you.

In learning how to make Big Decisions, my goal is not to help you make the "right" decision, because there usually isn't one. If there was, it would be easy to make. Instead, it's to help you make *great* decisions, each of which improves your life, and the lives of others, in a lasting way.

A dream is something you want to accomplish; a purpose you feel called to serve, or an inner change you want to make. It's a meaningful goal. It can be either external or internal, such as buying a new home for your family (an external goal), or being able to be more accepting and loving when your children are stressing you out (an internal goal).

Just like we have lots of small dilemmas to deal with each day, we also have lots of small goals that come up, such as wanting to respond to all our emails or get a healthy dinner on the table. The problem is that if we don't pay attention, these little goals can easily consume our lives.

If you want to lead an extraordinary life, you need to be able to slow down, connect with and commit to the Big Wins you want to create.

A *Big Win* is a meaningful, worthwhile goal, which has to meet three key characteristics. First, it is *heartfelt*. It matters to you. It's not just another item on a check list or another step on a ladder to success. It's a dream that lights you up and makes your heart sing. It's also *specific*. It's

YES YES HELL NO!

something measurable so you can know whether or not you've achieved it. And it's *scary*.

A *Big Win* is a meaningful goal that is heartfelt, specific and scary.

When a dream is both heartfelt and specific, it comes with a real emotional risk of failure. That naturally brings up our fears. And as strange as it might seem, so does the possibility of success. Big Wins pull us out of our comfort zone. They require change. And because of the way our nervous system is wired, positive changes can be just as scary as negative ones.

Like Big Decisions, each Big Win improves your life in a lasting way. By far, the most important step to creating a Big Win is the first step – your committed decision to go after it and put a heartfelt, specific and scary goal at stake.

Every Big Win starts with a Big Decision.

As an executive coach and leadership consultant, I'm in the business of helping people make Big Decisions and create Big Wins. Over the last decade, I've had the honor of working with a host of amazing clients, including corporate executives, best-selling authors, private equity magnates, and high flying entrepreneurs. I've also had the opportunity to help thousands of coaches, counselors, consultants and healers, in their quest to build their own purpose driven practice, where they get to both make money and make a difference while doing what they love.

In doing so, I've found that even the most successful people have areas where they feel insecure, inadequate or stuck. Even the strongest leaders have choices they struggle over and dreams they're afraid to own.

And even the wisest people regularly make decisions that *seem* rational – but aren't.

While we often think of ourselves as rational creatures, the bigger a dilemma is or the more important a dream is, the more our choices naturally become clouded by fear.

Have you ever turned down an exciting opportunity and instead played it safe? Have you ever made a decision out of anger and ended up hurting someone you love? Have you ever gotten so stressed that you went into survival mode and started obsessing over tiny things instead of focusing on the bigger picture? Or have you had times where you became addicted to achievement and approval?

I have. And pretty much everyone I know has done so, too. As we're going to discover in section three, there are many faces of fear and each shows up as a limitation – as a defect that distorts our decisions, sabotages our leadership, and holds us back from the things we most want in life.

However, we usually don't notice this. Like an iceberg, 90 percent of our fears remain out of sight, stored away in our unconscious mind. But that doesn't mean they're gone. Like trying

Daily Life

Insecurity
Arrogance
Stress
Procrastination
Silence
Violence

The Many Faces of Fear

to look through a layer of brown cooking grease that has been spread across a piece of glass, our hidden insecurities distorts our vision and colors our choices.

Instead of proclaiming themselves as such, our fears most commonly show up as innocent sounding statements that *sound* so reasonable – yet aren't.

Here's a quick test to see if this happens for you.

Do you ever find yourself saying any of the following?

"I'm upset because..."
"I need..."
"I should..."
"I shouldn't..."
"You shouldn't..."
"You must..."
"I'm stressed because..."
"I can't..."
"Yeah, I'd like to, but..."
"If I could just stop procrastinating, I would..."

If so, welcome to the human race. While each of these statements *can* be rational, they're almost always a sign that your choices aren't clean, and that your decisions are being distorted by your unconscious fears.

For example, I often find myself saying things like "I'm upset because I don't have more money." "I should be working harder." "Yeah, I'd like to go on a long beach vacation with the family, but I just don't have the time." And of course, "Sweetie, you don't understand, I *need* to buy more electronics!"

While these statements may sound reasonable, I've learned to recognize when they're really just symptoms of my hidden fears.

While this may sound disturbing, it's actually great news because the voice of fear can become one of your greatest allies – once you learn how to listen to it in a more effective way.

Chapter 3

The Three Voices

"Faust complained about having two souls in his breast, but I harbor a whole crowd of them and they quarrel. It is like being in a republic." ~ Otto von Bismarck

The problem with Big Wins and Big Decisions is that they bring up our inner fears and conflicts. "Which choice should I make?" "What if I fail?" "What if someone better comes along?" And of course, the ever present "I'm not worthy!"

The first step towards clarity is to recognize that the core conflict isn't between your different *choices:* it's between your different *voices.*

We all have different voices inside our heads. They're often in conflict. And when you learn how to resolve these conflicts, you're well on your way to getting more of what you most want in life.

This book is all about sorting out these voices.

"Multiple voices! What are you talking about?"

I know, I know. In our culture, the idea of conflicting inner voices tends to bring up visions of straitjackets and rubber rooms. One of my favorite T-shirts reads, "Don't worry. 9 of the 10 voices in my head say DON'T shoot."

Relax. We're not talking about multiple personality disorder – just healthy self-awareness.

In psychology, these different voices are called aspects or sub-personalities. Freud pointed out three big ones, which he called the id, the ego, and the super-ego. Jung added the collective unconscious to that list. Religious traditions have long taught the importance of listening to the voice of Spirit, also called the Holy Ghost. This is the proverbial "still, small voice."

So if it sometimes seems like there's a whole party going on inside your head, don't worry. You're not crazy. You're just waking up.

With training, most people can identify at least a dozen different sub-personalities, each of which is trying to serve them the best way it knows how. Having looked into my own, I've identified the Inner Critic, Little Brian, Teen Brian, Superior Sam, the Over-Achiever, and a host of others.

In terms of making Big Decisions (and sometimes even small ones), the three most important voices to discern are the voice of *fear*, the voice of *reason*, and the voice of *intuition*.

The voice of fear comes from the body. It's a basic emotional fight or flight response that can be traced all the way back to the reptilian brain. Its job is to warn us of anything that might be dangerous or cause us pain. While fear-based responses often seem *irrational*, they're actually *pre-rational*. Fear precedes reason. Where fear has been around for hundreds of millions of years, comes out of the limbic brain, and exists even in lizards, *reason* is a relative newcomer to the party.

The voice of reason comes from the mind, specifically from the neocortex. It's not emotional. It's a capacity for rational thought that analyzes pros and cons and makes rational decisions. The voice of reason's job is to be right, to find the correct answer or to make the best choice based on left-brain, logic-based intelligence. It's an extremely valuable tool, particularly when you learn how to combine it effectively with the voices of intuition and fear (which you are going to discover how to do in chapter 5).

The voice of intuition comes from spirit. Where the voice of fear is *pre-rational* and the voice of reason is *rational*, the voice of intuition is *trans-rational*. It exists beyond reason. That's why it seldom shows up in the form of thoughts or ideas. Instead, it acts more like a GPS device, helping us determine whether our choices are on course or not.

Where the voice of fear worries and the voice of reason analyzes, the voice of intuition resonates.

Intuition lights up around certain thoughts or decisions and not with others. It either offers a distinctly positive sensation or it goes thud.

The voice of intuition shows up most commonly as a feeling of joy, excitement, purpose or inspiration. For me, something that's "on course" lights me up – it pulls my awareness up towards my head and fills me with a feeling of joy. Something that's "off course" feels disconnected – it pulls my awareness down towards my feet and leaves me feeling empty. Then there are many things that don't seem to matter to the voice of intuition – they don't resonate one way or the other.

When Jenny came to me for coaching, her goal was to create a million-dollar business. Jenny is charming, funny and brilliant, and I was excited to explore how I could help her make it happen. Yet as she shared her vision, she didn't seem jazzed by it. There was no spark in her. So we explored some questions. "What would you do if you knew you could not fail?" "If you had a magic lamp with three wishes, what would you wish for?" "If you were giving a speech at your own funeral forty years from now, what would you want to say about your life?" I kept poking at her, asking every question in my bag of tricks.

After almost an hour of this, something shifted. Jenny stopped, took a breath, and with a tear in her eye, shared the following. "I've never told this to anyone else. I don't know if I've even admitted it to myself. What I really want is to be married and have a family. But I've given up believing that's possible for me."

That breakthrough made all the difference. In owning her truth, Jenny was able to start facing her fears, addressing her blocks, and claiming her dreams. She lost 40 pounds, reconnected with her birth mother, started acting in her local theatre, and began dating some wonderful men. She's transformed her self-confidence, built a community of close friends, and is now well on her way to creating a family of her own. All this happened because she was able to resolve this conflict between her inner voices and recognize that while her truth was saying "Yes Yes," her fear was saying "Hell No!"

The *Yes Yes Hell No!* tool empowers you to make Big Decisions and create Big Wins. It also serves a third purpose of releasing the fears that have been holding you back. When you're able to embrace the voice of fear, let it speak as itself, and genuinely listen to its warnings, a profound inner shift occurs. The voice of fear shifts from being an enemy to an ally, all those unconscious blocks and insecurities begin to fall away, and you're able to start taking action on your Big Decisions and Big Wins in much easier, more powerful, more graceful ways.

The key is being able to discern which voice is which and to allow each voice to speak as itself.

When Jenny shared about her business goals, my voice of intuition didn't light up at all. Her words fell flat – that thud I mentioned earlier – and left me with a slight feeling of disconnection. I just didn't get any sense that creating a big company was what she really cared about the most. So I kept asking questions until we got to what truly had energy for her – her desire to be married and have a family. When that happened, my intuition lit up as did hers, and we knew we were getting to something that really mattered to her.

The voice of intuition also shows up as a sense of direct knowing. Watch for it as you read this book. Notice when something just feels true to you. Not because of scientific studies or complicated arguments, but because somewhere inside, you just recognize it as wisdom. You resonate with the idea in a way that transcends logic.

That's the voice of intuition speaking.

Of the three voices, the voice of intuition is the surest guide to your highest good. It's the best advocate for your enlightened self-interest. It's a compass needle pointing directly toward your greatest joy.

The voice of intuition is always present, yet it can also be the most difficult voice to hear and the hardest voice to trust.

Thankfully, the voice of fear is easy to notice. It's rarely far away. It's loud and vocal. And it's extremely accurate – once you understand the language it speaks.

Chapter 4

When Comfort Becomes a Cage

"Life begins at the end of your comfort zone."
~ Neale Donald Walsch

To an animal, any change can signify danger. A bright light, a sharp noise, a movement in the brush – anything unexpected is a cause for alarm.

Similarly, to the voice of fear, all change is scary. It doesn't matter if it's a good change or a bad change: different is dangerous. It's uncomfortable. It's everywhere you don't want to be.

Your comfort zone consists of all the things in life that you've already experienced and become okay living with on a daily basis. The skills you've mastered? Comfortable. The success you've achieved? Comfortable. The friends you've connected with? Comfortable.

Anything new you want? Uncomfortable.

Just because something feels comfortable doesn't mean that it's healthy or good. Have you ever put off a relationship break-up even though you knew it was time to end it? Or held on to a job that you hated just because you needed the paycheck?

Over time human beings can get used to just about anything, to the point where it can actually feel safer to stay in an abusive relationship than to leave it for something new.

When it comes to the things you most want, like good health, wealth, love, and happiness, your comfort zone sets the limit: both on how bad you'll let your life get before you make a change, and on how good you'll allow it to be.

This is why sudden wealth can create such misery. It's why so many famous people get addicted to drugs. And it's why the last five years of my marriage have been so difficult for me.

Not because the relationship has been so bad, but because it's been so good.

My mother died when I was three, in what was easily the most painful experience of my life. By all accounts, she was a remarkable woman – beautiful, loving, charming, and kind. And then I lost her. One day she was my everything; the next day she was gone. Her death left me with a deep wound and a profound fear of abandonment. At an almost cellular level, I learned that love is everything – and that love is loss. So as I became an adult, finding someone to love became both my greatest desire and my  greatest fear. Like Jenny, I wanted more than anything else to be married and have a family. Yet deep down I didn't believe it was possible. I didn't believe I deserved it. And I feared that if I did manage to find love, it would be taken from me again.

Mind you, for most of my life I didn't really know what was really going on inside me. I didn't realize why I had such deep feelings of unworthiness, why I was so obsessed with finding The One, or why I was so incapable of staying in a relationship for more than a few months.

When my mother died, her loss was so intense, and I had so few tools to deal with it, that I completely repressed the experience. My father remarried six months later to an amazing woman named Zina. I bonded to her and buried the wound away. I grew up in a remarkably loving and happy family, with a mother who fully treated my sister and I as if we were her own. So as a young adult, if someone asked me who was in the picture on my desk, I'd share "That's my birth mother Renée. She died when I was too young to remember her." And that was my honest truth. I didn't have a single emotional or mental memory of her.

Except it was a lie. What I didn't realize yet was the wound wasn't gone. It was waiting. It was sitting below the surface, in anticipation of the day when I'd finally be able to open it up and heal it.

What I didn't realize yet was that it would take a major emotional crisis, a spiritual awakening, and six years of full time inner work for me to heal this wound to the point where I could actually be in relationship.

And what I didn't realize yet was that I would have to go through three experiences of sabotaging and almost destroying my relationship with Nicole, before I could open my heart enough to actually feel her love for me and my love for her.

With all the challenges we faced, it was truly a cause for celebration when we gathered our families on a Santa Barbara beach that beautiful August day, and the two of us (finally!) said "I do."

Marrying Nicole and creating a family with her is the greatest achievement of my life. Not just because it's one of the best things I've done, but also because it's required the most work.

I couldn't have done it without the power of this simple, powerful little tool. Each twist and turn in my path was marked by a clear and unmistakable *Yes Yes Hell No!* Even when I didn't fully realize it, it was this tool that became my most trusted compass. It was the guidance that steered me through each storm.

And I continue to need its guidance. The amount of love I have in my life scares me. A lot. It's definitely not comfortable. Every day, Nicole and our girls stretch the boundaries of what I can receive. They push me to open my heart. They challenge me to take a risk. And each day my fears tell me to close back up, to sabotage the relationship. To try and find a way to make things feel safe.

Some days I listen to my fears, but most days I don't. Again, not because there's something special about me, but because there's something special about the way I've learned to make decisions. My life keeps getting better and better because somewhere along the way I discovered a deep truth.

In the absence of a real and present danger, the voice of fear is an almost perfect indicator of which direction to go – as long as you head the other way.

Whenever you hear the voice of fear, it's telling you one of two things. Either it's warning you about a real and present danger, or it's alerting you to an opportunity for growth and change. It's letting you know that something just registered on an inner sensor and your life is at risk of getting either better or worse.

The problem is the voice of fear can't tell which is which.

And in today's day and age, the opportunities for growth tend to vastly outweigh the real dangers.

A thousand years ago, each day was a gamble. Human survival depended on listening to our fears. While there were surely opportunities for growth and courage, in most cases discretion truly was the better part of valor. It was all anyone could do just to feed their families and keep them safe.

Today, if you have a stable job in a first-world country, your children are more likely to suffer from obesity than starvation. You're more likely to die from heart disease than violence. And given the exponential pace of change today, if you're not scared of growth, well, you're just not paying attention.

If you're walking through a bad part of town and someone comes at you with a knife – run. However, if you're worried about making the wrong choice or failing to achieve your dreams – pause. Don't take your fears at face value. They still have something important to tell you, but listen carefully: it's probably not what you think.

"Most of us believe that we will finally feel satisfied and content with our lives when we get the good news we have been waiting for, find a healthy relationship, or achieve one of our personal goals. However, this rarely happens. Good fortune is often followed by negative emotions that overtake us and result in destructive behaviors."

"This is the one problem that holds you back. I call it the Upper Limit Problem, and I haven't met a person yet who didn't suffer at least a little bit from it. Even if you're already extravagantly successful, I can promise you that your own version of the Upper Limit Problem is still holding you back from achieving your true potential."

~ Gay Hendricks, The Big Leap

Chapter 5

Yes Yes Hell No!

"The hardest thing about the road not taken is that you never know where it might have led." ~ Lisa Wingate

With that setup, you're now ready to learn a surefire tool for creating Big Wins and making Big Decisions. It's guaranteed to help you make a great decision, every time. Again, we're not talking about how to make the *right* decision, because with important dreams and dilemmas there usually isn't one. Instead, let your goal be to make *great* decisions. This tool will help you do so.

The *Yes Yes Hell No!* tool for making great decisions will not let you down. It's reliable, durable, and requires no down payment. Your life can get even better and shine even brighter than you're currently capable of imagining – if you learn and apply this simple technology.

But beware! While it's an incredibly *positive* tool, it's not always *comfortable*. Used carefully and consistently, it will improve your life in profound and concrete ways. You'll discover your dreams, fulfill your purpose, create amazing relationships, and experience great success. Yet these gifts come with a challenge. It's not an overwhelming challenge, but one that must be met: you must develop the habit of moving out of your comfort zone and through your fears.

Are you ready for this life-changing tool?

Here it is.

The surest way to make a great decision is to look for the choice that evokes these three internal responses: the voice of intuition lights up, the voice of reason checks it out and approves it, and the voice of fear says, "Hell No! Run away!"

Whenever your three voices say, *Yes Yes Hell No!* – go forward. You're making a great decision. You're on your soul's path.

Great choices are both inspiring and scary. They cause your intuition to light up and your heart to sing. At the same time, they bring up your fears. And the bigger the opportunity, the louder and trickier the voice of fear becomes.

The key is to listen for the three voices, discern which is which, and respond accordingly.

Three of the most important Big Decisions in my life were my choices to move to California, to leave my career in Silicon Valley for six years of full time growth and healing, and to open my heart to the love of my life.

In all three cases, my voice of intuition said "Yes!" When I thought about going to graduate school in California, my heart lit up. Each time I explored the idea of doing more healing work, it felt like I was coming home. And each time I was able to actually feel the love that was in my heart for Nicole, I lit up like a Christmas tree.

In all three situations, my voice of reason confirmed my choice. Berkeley was one of four schools tied for the number one ranking in Computer Science. In leaving Silicon Valley, I both had enough money to do so, and I'd realized that I absolutely had to do this inner work if I was to be capable of creating the loving family that was so important to me. And with Nicole, our list of core values and priorities matched up in remarkable ways.

And with all three choices, my voice of fear screamed out a big, fat "Hell No!" In applying to only the two California schools, there was a very real risk that I'd be rejected by both. And if I was accepted, it meant leaving behind a very safe and comfortable environment, for something that was profoundly new and unknown.

Leaving behind my career as a Silicon Valley entrepreneur was terrifying. At that point, I could have easily raised millions for another start up. I was interviewing for executive positions at public technology companies. I was on the fast track to wealth beyond my dreams. Growing up in Illinois, my goal had been to eventually make $60,000 a year as an engineer. Now it seemed like I had received the winning ticket for the lottery, and was thinking of throwing it all away.

Yet even with all the inner work I did, opening my heart to Nicole was the scariest choice of them all. It evoked deep, unconscious, almost death level fears. It caused me to sabotage our courtship repeatedly. It made it excruciatingly difficult to hear my intuition. It was like the mother of all final exams.

If it hadn't been for a series of last minute, outside interventions, I would have backed away from this tool, sabotaged my dreams, and walked away from the love of my life.

Three times.

As I regularly tell my wife and daughters, their love is the great miracle of my life.

So how can we help you learn this life changing tool?

It all starts by connecting with a dream or a dilemma: a Big Win you want to create or a Big Decision you want to make. Then the next step is to connect with your fears, because it's usually easiest to start with the loudest voice first.

Which choices scare you? What are all the reasons you might *not* want to do something? Let the voice of fear have its say. You don't need to *fight* it or make it wrong. You don't need to *flee* from it or pretend it's not there. And you don't need to *feed* it or focus on it and give it energy. Instead, just listen.

When you try to fight, flee, or feed your fears, they only get stronger. Yet when you *embrace* them, they begin to drop away.

The voice of fear is here to serve you the best way it knows how. Its purpose isn't to *stop you* from moving forward: it's to *warn you* of potential dangers. Listen directly to this voice and give it a chance to speak as the voice of fear, rather than it needing to masquerade as something else. Once you've listened, it tends to quiet down and let you get on with life. It also becomes much easier to detect. As you learn to listen to the voice of fear and meet it with both acceptance and courage, it gets softer. It stops needing to be so clever. It can actually become your friend.

The next step is to hear the voice of intuition. This is much easier to do once you've talked to your fears and listened for every "Hell No!" you can find. To connect with your intuition, feel into the different options. Imagine yourself making a choice and then notice what sensations show up in your body. What lights you up? What inspires you? What makes your heart sing? Is there a balancing "Yes" for the original "Hell No!?" If you're not clear about this voice yet, don't worry. I'll give you plenty of tools for deepening your understanding of it.

Once you've connected to the voices of fear and intuition, then it's time to bring in the voice of reason. In making great decisions the voice of reason plays three roles. Its first job is to provide a sanity check. Moving out of our comfort zone is scary. It often feels like a dive into the great unknown. Reason's first job is to verify that you're not dealing with a real and present danger. While it may *feel* like a cliff, is it an *actual* cliff? This doesn't mean waiting until you know how things are going to work out. It's not about trying to control the outcome. It's about looking for choices that are both inspiring and scary, and then checking to make sure that they're also sane.

Its second job is to prioritize your choices. As you start to master this tool, you'll find yourself discovering more and more *Yes Yes Hell No!* opportunities. Which ones are most important? Which ones are aligned with your deepest values and highest priorities?

The voice of reason's third job is to ground your decisions and help you move forward in the most efficient and effective way. Once you've decided *what* you want to do, reason's job is to help you decide *how* to do it. Rather than taking no risks or crazy ones, how can you craft a path that, while it may feel scary, is also safe?

I often work with people who have found their calling and are committed to creating a purpose-driven career. They may want to be a coach, a counselor, an inspirational speaker, or a healer. Yet they also need to pay their bills. Their dream is to create a business that allows them to both make money and make a difference. However, from the beginning they usually have no idea of what this really entails and many of them fail. Instead of creating a purpose driven *career*, they often end up with either a *hobby* or a *cliff dive*. Either they play things safe and never really take the plunge, or they take naïve risks, dive off a cliff and get hurt.

I regularly connect with courageous cliff divers who have quit their jobs, followed their hearts, invested their savings, maxed out their credit cards – and are on the edge of failure. They've created huge amounts of *personal growth*, but not nearly as much *success*. They've demonstrated plenty of *courage*, but not as much *effectiveness*. They've done nothing wrong, but making decisions this way often leads to suffering.

I took a cliff dive when I started that internet software company as my first job out of college. I learned more in four short years than I would have imagined possible, but even though I had the best intentions, I also hurt a lot of people and made a lot of promises that I wasn't able to keep. Today, I wouldn't trade that experience for anything. It was a period of profound growth that laid the foundation for much of my subsequent success.

But I can't say I recommend that route. There were wiser, easier choices I could have made. My failure left behind some deep wounds and a number of ruined relationships. That doesn't mean it was the wrong choice – but it may well have been the hardest.

Growth is scary, but it doesn't have to be dangerous. It bears repeating that a path can be both inspiring, scary and safe. Instead of looking at things from an all-or-nothing perspective, the voice of reason is a great tool for creating stair steps of growth and success. Armed with courage and wisdom, you can train on the one meter diving board and then move to the three and ten meter boards before you start looking for the big cliffs.

Chapter 6

Which Pill Do You Want to Take?

"Our dilemma is that we hate change and love it at the same time; what we really want is for things to remain the same but get better." ~ Sydney J. Harris

Now that you have an idea of what we're talking about, it's time to make a decision regarding what you want to get out of reading this book.

There are two reasons to read this book. The first is to learn something interesting about life. The second is to change the way you actually live it.

You can use this book to gain *information* or to create *transformation*. You can make it a mental exercise or an ongoing practice to change your life for the better.

It's like the choice in the movie *The Matrix* between taking the red pill or the blue pill.

The blue pill is comfortable. It lets us go back to sleep. It doesn't rock the boat, and it keeps your life the same as it's always been.

The red pill creates change. It's different. It's uncomfortable. Sometimes it's scary. Occasionally it's terrifying. The good news is that it's the fast track to creating everything you most want in life. The bad news is that it requires you to step outside of your comfort zone and do something different.

Either choice is fine, but you must choose. And the first step in using this new technology is to get clear on which choice you want to make.

So take a minute and allow yourself to dream. Stretch your conception of what is possible for your life. What would you do if you could create miraculous growth and change in your life? What would you wish for if you had a sure fire tool for finding and living your purpose? What dreams would you open your heart to, if you knew you could not fail?

Sit with these questions. Open your heart. And then decide.

With this book, is your intention to learn new ideas and concepts? Or do you want to use it to create lasting change? If the latter, are you willing to leave your comfort zone and face your fears?

Again – either choice is fine. You can use this book for either purpose. You might even read it through once for information, then check in and see if it resonates. If so, you could go through it again and use the tools and exercises to start creating transformation.

The key is to make a conscious choice.

Circle your choice.

Blue Pill: My intention is to learn new information

Red Pill: My intention is to create transformation

If you chose the Blue Pill, terrific. Please read this book as you would any other. Feel free to circle any chapters that you think you might want to come back to later and explore in more depth.

If you chose the Red Pill, that's also terrific. As a first step, if you haven't done so already, please go to *www.YesYesHellNo.com* and download the complimentary accompanying workbook. Print it out and respond to the questions and exercises as you go along.

Chapter 7

What Big Decisions Would You Like to Make?

"Choices are the hinges of destiny." ~ Edwin Markham

In this first exercise, you'll look at some of the current choices you're facing. These choices primarily fall into two categories: dreams and dilemmas. You'll explore your dilemmas in this chapter and your dreams in the next – what we're calling your *Big Decisions* and your *Big Wins*.

Of these two types of choices, dilemmas are the most obvious. They're the decisions you agonize over when you have to choose between two paths and you don't know which one to take. A dilemma can usually be phrased as an either/or question.

"Do I want to stick with my current career *or* try something that feels more on purpose?" "Do I want to live here *or* move somewhere else?" "Do I want to get married to this person *or* not?" "Do I want to have a child *or* focus on career and travel?" "Do I want to apply for a promotion *or* wait until the next progress review comes through?"

You know a choice is a Big Decision when it meets two criteria: the outcome matters to you, and you feel emotionally conflicted about the alternatives. Usually, a Big Decision triggers your fears in some way. And the best way to make a Big Decision is to look for the option that shows up as a *Yes Yes Hell No*!

Choosing whether or not to marry Nicole wasn't just a single Big Decision for me. It was a whole series of them. Three of which I very nearly managed to permanently screw up.

Even after a tremendous amount of personal growth and healing work, with dozens of the best coaches, counselors, healers and teachers I could find, I still had a deep wound over my birth mother's death. And I still had some deep, paralyzing fears of abandonment.

So it was only natural that on our third date, I sat her down and explained the facts of our situation to her. "Nicole, I really like you. I think you're beautiful, funny, brilliant and charming. I'd really like to date you. Let's be honest. I'd really like to have sex with you. But before we do so, you need to know one thing. You're not The One, and we won't be getting married together."

To which she replied, "what is *wrong* with you!?"

Thankfully, Nicole is much smarter, wiser and more intuitive than I am. She saw right through me. She recognized my fears for what they were. And she was able to see just how good a fit we could be for each other. (Mind you, I still tell her that I was just playing hard to get, as part of my brilliant plan to win her over. But for some reason, she's still not buying it.)

That said, after three months of this, Nicole got clear that it was time for us to step up or step out. It was either time for us to become exclusive, or to break up. She sat me down and explained the facts of our situation, and for the first of three times, I almost walked away. My voice of fear tried to sabotage things, by masquerading as the voice of reason. It asked me "Wouldn't it be smarter if you kept your options open?"

So I negotiated.

I asked her, "What do you mean by exclusive? Would it count if I dated other women but didn't have sex with them? What if I limited things to just kissing them?"

To which she replied, "what is *wrong* with you?!"

And thankfully, I was able to see my fears for what they were. I was able to sense at least enough of my intuition to get a sense that this relationship might be a good fit for me. And my mind was able to run through my checklist of values and must-haves, and see that she fit one every one of them. So I committed to that next step – and thank God that I did.

What defines a Big Decision is not the size of the choice but the size of the emotions that come up around making the choice. For example, Big Decisions often show up in relationships, around how we respond when someone we love does something that makes us feel defensive or angry. When this happens, do you respond with anger? Do you pull away? Or do you find a way to breathe into your feelings, embrace the conflict, and turn the emotions into opportunities for personal growth? These choices can show up on a daily basis, and how you respond is one of the strongest predictors of relationship success and lasting happiness.

We face many smaller dilemmas each day. In this case, the stakes may not be as high, but the tool works just the same. "Do I want to vent my anger at someone or take some deep breaths?" "Do I want to go to the gym or relax on the couch?" "Do I want to tell my husband how wonderful he is or give him a back rub?" (Honey, are you reading this?)

At a deep level, most of us have been trained to avoid conflict. We tend to judge it as a sign that something is wrong or that we're off course. Yet when it's a particular type of conflict – where you're experiencing a *Yes Yes Hell*

No! around a Big Decision that you're seeking to make – that feeling of inner conflict can be one of the most trustworthy signs that you're exactly on course.

So take a minute. What are some of the Big Decisions, large and small, which you'd most like to make?

Then take a big, deep breath. When you breathe deeply, fear starts turning into excitement. And excitement is a great thing to be feeling as you read the next chapter, where we're going to look at your dreams and start exploring the Big Wins you want to create.

As a reminder, if you picked the Red Pill, please visit www.YesYesHellNo.com to download your complimentary workbook which contains the full version of this exercise as well as a study guide and the complete exercises for each chapter of this book.

Chapter 8

What Big Wins Would You Like to Create?

"Only those who will risk going too far can possibly find out how far one can go." ~ T.S. Eliot

Where dilemmas can be painful, dreams tend to be both exciting and scary. Where dilemmas are about making *Big Decisions*, dreams are about creating *Big Wins*.

Dreams are something positive you want to create, discover, or achieve. They involve either a *direction* in life or a *destination* along the way. A direction engages your core values, such as love, joy, integrity or freedom. Directional dreams are ultimately about whom you're *being* in life and how you want that to change over time. For example, "I want to become more joyful and loving" might be one of your goals.

Destinations involve what you want to *have* or *do*. For example, "I want to double my income" or "I want to take my family on a vacation to Fiji."

Like Big Decisions, Big Wins involve high stakes. They're heartfelt goals that also trigger our fears and bring up an inner conflict – a *Yes Yes Hell No!*

A Big Win is heartfelt, specific, and scary. First off, a Big Win is *heartfelt*. It's energizing. It excites you. It's in alignment with your purpose and your path.

A Big Win is also *specific*. While it's rooted in a direction you want to go, a Big Win also includes specific destinations along the way so you can gauge your progress and celebrate your success.

Finally, a Big Win is *scary*. When you connect to a goal that truly means something to you, and then make it specific enough that it becomes real and tangible, this automatically brings up your fears. It pulls you outside of your comfort zone in a very clear and profound way.

Big Wins and Big Decisions often go hand in hand. For example, I probably wouldn't be a husband and father today if I hadn't sat down thirteen years ago, owned the fact that getting married and having a family was both one of my greatest desires and greatest fears, and turned marriage into a Big Win that I was fully committed to creating. It was that clarity and commitment that propelled me into doing the necessary inner work with my fears and childhood wounding, so that I was actually able to make a series of Big Decisions when Nicole came along.

So what are the Big Wins you want to create?

Pick a Big Win that excites you in each of three areas: work, relationships and self.

Now take a look at your answers. As you ponder them, how much do your dreams excite you? Are they heartfelt, specific and scary?

When you do this exercise for the first time, it can be hard to fully claim your dreams. That's natural. The more you care about something, the more challenging it can be to truly acknowledge and own that dream. After all, what if you really went for it and then failed?

It takes courage to go after what you really most want in life.

Do you remember the story of Jenny? Like me, her dream was to be married and have a family, yet this terrified her. Rather than go for what she wanted most, it felt safer for her to settle. She gave up and then started telling herself stories about all the other, smaller things she could go after instead.

Thankfully, my experience in creating my own Big Wins gave me the capacity to support her, as we helped her turn around, discover her *Yes Yes Hell No!*, declare her Big Win, make friends with her fears, and start taking committed action towards her most heartfelt, specific and scary goal.

Chapter 9

How to Release Your Fears and Experience Freedom

"Every positive change – every jump to a higher level of energy and awareness – involves a rite of passage. Each time to ascend to a higher rung on the ladder of personal evolution, we must go through a period of discomfort, of initiation. I have never found an exception."
~ Dan Millman

If all we did was teach you how to find your fears and do the opposite of what they say, this could make for a very difficult, frightening and painful path.
Thankfully, it doesn't have to be that way.

The first step in using this tool involves getting clear on the Big Wins you want to create and the Big Decisions you want to make. Then the second step involves releasing the fears that have been holding you back by using a revolutionary tool for letting go of fear.

When you do so, the *Yes Yes Hell No!* turns into a Yes Yes Yes, where all three voices line up and start pointing in the same direction. This creates an almost miraculous sense of freedom, as you shift from feeling like you have one foot on the gas and one on the brake, to a place where you have full control over how fast you go. When this happens you're in a state of Flow, which we're going explore more in Chapter

16. It's a great gift, and one that we're going to teach you how to access at will.

The key to this process is to make the shift from fighting, fleeing or feeding your fears to embracing them. In it, you shift from trying to conquer and eliminate your fears, to accepting and understanding them. You literally build a relationship with the voice of fear, seek to understand how it's serving you the best way it knows how, and turn it into a friend.

In doing so, it's important to understand that there are two types of courage and that they play very different roles. The masculine form of courage involves determination and commitment, and its primary role is to help us overcome external obstacles. For example, I have a cousin who is a Green Beret, currently serving his third tour of duty in Afghanistan. Dedicated to serving our country, he is one of the most powerful examples of masculine courage that I've ever met.

Yet as a legion of homeless veterans can attest, the courage it takes to fight is very different from the courage it takes to heal. What's required for survival is often the opposite of what's required for growth. And when you believe that courage always involves conquering, your capacity for change becomes stunted.

Where the *courage to conquer* requires determination, the *courage to change* is based in acceptance.

One of the core principles of psychology is Carl Jung's "What you resist, persists." While you can kill an enemy, you can't kill your fears. Violence is just another manifestation of fear, and when you try to bulldoze your way through your insecurities it only makes them stronger. You may be able to drive them underground – for a time – but sooner or later they come back with a vengeance.

The feminine version of courage involves acceptance and forgiveness, and its primary role is to help us release internal conflicts.

Creating an extraordinary life requires developing both determination and acceptance.

When faced with your insecurities, notice the three defaults you typically choose from. Do you tend to fight your fears by making them wrong and trying to eliminate them? Do you tend to avoid your fears by numbing out, distracting yourself, or sweeping conflicts under the rug? Or do you tend to feed them by playing the victim and focusing on all the things that aren't going well instead of the ones that are thriving?

By far, these are the most common approaches, yet none of them work.

True change starts with listening to your fears. It starts with giving the voice of fear the opportunity to speak as itself, as fear, rather than needing to pretend that it's the voice of truth. And it starts by meeting the voice of fear with acceptance and understanding, where you listen to its concerns without judgment or fear.

When you give yourself to this deep listening and the voice of fear feels that its warnings have been heard, it releases much of its energy.

Then as you continue the process of *Making Friends With Your Fears*, which you will be learning in chapter 32, something magical happens. As you meet your fears with love instead of fear, with acceptance instead of judgment, your fears shift from being an enemy – stuck on the other side of an inner battle – to being a friend. The war ends and all your three voices start pulling together.

When this happens, everything changes. You become radically more powerful. You experience a deep sense of inner freedom. Patterns of anxiety, insecurity and even depression start to disappear. And your life improves in remarkable ways.

For me, I had a deep experience of this dynamic the second time I almost derailed my courtship of Nicole. (Yes ladies, I did buy her a large diamond for her engagement ring, and I also recognize that I still have a *lot* of penance to go.)

After a year of dating, while I had committed to being exclusive, I still hadn't let go of my story that "you're not The One." And I still was using that story to keep my distance, whenever things got too scary. Finally, after one fight too many, she'd had enough. She let me know that she loved me. She wanted to be with me. And she couldn't handle my avoidance any longer. I needed to either open my heart and decide that she was the one, or let her go.

To my credit, I really heard her, and I was beginning to realize by this point how much I actually loved her. But no matter how hard I tried, I just couldn't get past my fears. So I asked her for a week to be alone, and really sit with the decision.

A week turned into two. I meditated. I prayed. I called on everyone in my team of coaches, counselors and healers. I worked really hard to get clear, but no matter what I did, it didn't feel right. After developing increasing trust in my ability to listen to and trust my voice of intuition, I just couldn't get a clear *Yes Yes Hell No!* The fear was certainly present, and the relationship made sense from a rational point of view, but I just couldn't feel that inner sense of intuitive knowing I had come to trust so well.

I couldn't get to a clear yes, so I decided I needed to end things. I was getting ready to call Nicole and break up for good, when my father called. My parents are very respectful of boundaries, and rarely offer unsolicited advice. Yet in this case, my father felt compelled to reach out and share the following wisdom.

"Brian, ever since your mother died, there has been a titanium wall around your heart, which has kept out everyone but myself and your sister Shauna. Even your new mother, brother and sister haven't been able to get in. I don't know if Nicole is The One for you or not. But I do know that she is one of the very few people I've met who could help you take down this wall. I have this sense that she is a gift from your mother and from God, to help you do so, and that if you pass up this gift, you may not get another opportunity like this for a very long time."

My father's words resonated deeply. And in listening to him, I realized I'd been focused on the wrong Big Decision. I'd been asking the wrong question. Since our first date, I'd been trying to decide if Nicole was The One – I'd been trying to decide if she was the Big Win I had been waiting for. But this was premature. I couldn't love anyone the way I wanted to, without first letting down the wall around my heart. All the years of inner work had been in preparation for this moment. I'd created enough cracks in the wall, done enough healing work, and practiced enough self-acceptance, to be able to commit to making one of the biggest changes of my life.

So instead of committing to marry Nicole, or deciding to break up with her, I shared my truth. "Nicole, I have this wall around my heart. I want more than anything to pull down this wall, and I believe you are someone who I can do that with. I can't commit to you being The One, because I can't yet know whether or not that's true for me. But I know that answer lives on the other side of this wall, and I'm willing to commit to do whatever it takes to take the wall down in my relationship with you."

In response, Nicole asked if my commitment included being willing to go to a marriage therapist with her. My response. "Sure, but can't go back to having sex for a few weeks first?"

Yes, I know. For someone who can be so smart sometimes, I can also be really, really stupid as well.

Between my father's wisdom and Nicole's love, I was able to muster up the courage to change. I was able to accept my fears, at an even deeper level. I was able to commit to receiving support. And I was able to open my heart. Of course, there was still a third time before we got married when I almost managed to destroy the relationship. And there was the the profound lesson about love I learned in doing so. But this was the turning point, and as proud as I am of my work in the relationship, my father definitely deserves credit – and my gratitude – for the assist.

In responding to the voice of fear, both types of courage are important. Internal change starts with acceptance, where you make friends with your fears, and then moves to commitment, where you make a strong decision to move forward and receive support, in ways that are both scary and safe.

In contrast, dealing with external dangers is simpler. If it's a real and present danger, fight or flight are the natural choices.

The key is to learn what is most important for each situation. It's to learn the difference between a *Tiger, Wall, or Leap of Faith.*

Chapter 10

Tiger, Wall, or Leap of Faith?

"Follow your bliss. If you do follow your bliss, you put yourself on a kind of track that has been there all the while waiting for you, and the life you ought to be living is the one you are living." ~ Joseph Campbell

When you notice yourself feeling scared, insecure, or upset – pay attention. The voice of fear has something to tell you and it does intend to be clear. It's just that when it's on high alert, the voice of fear doesn't have a particularly large vocabulary.

"Danger!" "Warning!" "Stay back!"

The more primal the fears are, the less nuanced the conversation is going to be. Even more challenging, from one situation to another, the same words can mean very different things. Sometimes the voice of fear is warning about a Tiger. Sometimes it's letting you know that you've hit a Wall. And other times it's pointing to a Leap of Faith.

A Tiger is a real and present danger. If you're in a dark alley and someone is walking towards you with a knife – run! This is where the courage to conquer is just what's needed.

I once faced a Tiger while water skiing and it almost killed me. I was out on the lake with a bunch of friends being pulled behind the boat. The driver wanted to drop me in front of the houseboat where we were staying. So he pulled a tight circle, expecting me to cut across the *inside* of the turn and drop in front of the houseboat. I misunderstood and went to the *outside* of the turn, in a "crack the whip" move instead.

Picture me flying in a circle at 50 miles per hour, with no control over my direction, hanging on as tight as I can to the tow bar, when the voice of fear yells, "WATCH OUT!" Looking up, I see that I've called it wrong and I'm about to hit the side of the houseboat at full speed.

Not good. Real danger.

With no time to think, I dropped the rope, planted the ski sideways, and fell backward in an emergency stop. At that point, it was the only action that could have saved me, and it did just that. While I hit the boat with a huge thump and kicked up an enormous wave of water that doused the sunbathers on the roof, I came away unscathed.

Thank you, fear!

	Intuition	Reason	Fear
Tiger	No	No	**Hell No!**
Wall	No	Yes	
Leap of Faith	Yes	Yes	

Fear's primary job is to keep you safe. If you're facing a Tiger, listen to the warning and take action.

Where a Tiger indicates a real and present danger, a Leap of Faith offers an opportunity for growth in which you're called to develop the courage to change. So how do you tell them apart?

When you're facing a Tiger, all three voices agree. There's no argument. If it's a real and present danger, all three voices will call out in sync: "No, No, Hell No!"

It's pretty straightforward.

The thing is, unless you're on a safari (or working in a war zone) Tigers just aren't that common anymore. Nowadays when the voice of fear shows up, you're much more likely to be facing a Leap of Faith. In that case, while the voice of fear says "Run away," the voices of intuition and reason say, "Go forward." So when you put the three voices together, what you get is *Yes Yes Hell No!*

That's the golden combination. When that happens, go forward. You're making a great decision.

So what happens if the voices of intuition and reason disagree?

Sometimes, the voice of reason says, "Go forward," but the voice of intuition disagrees. It's not that it says no; it just doesn't light up. It doesn't applaud the choice, or make your heart sing. When this happens, you've hit a Wall, and your best bet is to look for other options.

In the case of choices you've already made, you know you've hit a Wall when you're stuck. You're in a situation where you're committed to a goal and you're putting in lots of effort, but you're not making much progress. You're swimming against the current instead of cooperating with the flow. For no apparent reason, things are a lot harder than you'd expect them to be.

Walls often show up when you start living life according to all the things you think you *should* be doing or *have* to be doing, instead of the things that you truly *choose* to be doing – those that truly align with your highest values.

When Andrew first came to see me, he was making millions as an investment banker. From the outside, it looked like he had it all: a gorgeous wife, a Stanford MBA, terrific children, a huge house, a beautiful car, and vacations all over the world. Yet inside he felt miserable. He was acting out in addictive ways, his relationship with his wife was falling apart, he didn't want to get out of bed most days, and he hated his work.

For more than twenty years, Andrew had lived his life trying to measure up to other people's expectations. He'd gotten really good at doing all the things he thought he should be doing, but he'd never stopped to figure out who he was and what he really wanted. Andrew had done all the right things in his quest to feel worthy, but no matter how hard he tried it was never enough.

He'd hit a Wall, and he needed to change. Instead of listening to his fears of unworthiness, he needed to locate and listen to the voice of his heart.

While Walls can bring on insecurity or unworthiness, their most common symptom is frustration. Frustration and anger are two of the many faces of fear – they're the "fight" side of our fight-or-flight reaction. They feel different from fear, but they come from the same source.

Like a Leap of Faith, a Wall signals an opportunity for learning and growth. The difference is that a Leap of Faith ushers you forward, while a Wall tells you to change course.

They often go hand in hand. If you've hit a Wall, chances are good there's a Leap of Faith you've been avoiding. Andrew's Leap of Faith first required that he let go of his need for others' approval. Instead of carrying on trying to do the right thing, thus living his life according to others' expectations, he needed to slow down and examine his true desires. What did he want? What made him happy? What were his highest values? What made his heart sing?

Over the course of the following year, Andrew made a series of deep changes. He negotiated a graceful, two-year exit plan from the firm he'd helped create. He started exploring some new, more fulfilling career options. He opened up to his wife about his feelings, and they started growing together again. As a couple, they started planning the next stage of their life together. Today, Andrew meets his challenges more directly and he no longer feels stuck. He's excited to get out of bed each day, he's growing in fulfilling ways, and he loves his life again.

Walls show up in many different ways. For Andrew, the Wall showed up internally, as a deep sense of unhappiness. For Steve, the Wall manifested more concretely as a lack of external results.

Steve was the CEO of a large technology firm when he hired Larry to come in and help turn his company around. When Larry came on board, the stock price had declined for five consecutive quarters, employee engagement scores were low, and the other members of the executive team were at one another's throats. The company had clearly hit a Wall.

So Steve ordered 360-degree evaluations for all the leaders in the company – except himself, because he was "too busy to participate." What he couldn't see was that his leadership was a large part of the problem.

While Steve seemed to be in charge, his fears were really running the show. While he thought of himself as confident, others saw him as both insecure and arrogant. ("My team is the problem and I'm the solution.") And while he was working as hard as he could, his overstress and chronic "busyness" kept him from being able to even see, let alone fix, the real problems in his firm.

Steve had hit a Wall and needed to look for his Leap of Faith. He was getting strong feedback that he needed to change direction. He needed to get help, explore his blind spots, and develop his leadership in a few key areas.

A few people, including Larry, had the courage to point out some of his problems, along with some of his opportunities for growth and deep change. Unfortunately, he was too scared, too stressed, or too arrogant to make these changes, and after eight months and another large round of layoffs, he was fired by his board.

When you hit a Wall, there's a lesson to learn. You may need to change course, focus on what you really want, or learn how to work smarter instead of harder. Sometimes the lesson is obvious – at least to those around you – and sometimes it can be tricky. Either way, if you're hitting a Wall, where reason says yes but intuition says no, it's time to look for a Leap of Faith.

I've hit far more Walls in my life than I care to admit. If my life as a twenty-something were drawn as a cartoon, it would depict a series of brick walls with Brian-shaped imprints in them.

For me, it's clear that my most persistent Walls had to do with the lessons I needed to learn about love.

For a long time I thought I was single because I lacked enough achievements. But the real problem was an excess of fear. In my attempts to achieve my way to love, I kept hearing the voice of fear and believing it was truth. "I don't feel worthy, but if I'm successful enough, then I'll find The One. She'll fall in love with me and we'll live happily ever after." That was my guiding principle for a good dozen years.

There was just one little problem: it was utterly untrue.

The reality was that love terrified me. I thought I was seeking perfection, but what I really wanted was protection. A more honest statement of my motivations would have been "As long as I'm so busy proving my worth, I don't need to slow down, open my heart, and risk getting hurt. I don't need to face my fears and take a Leap of Faith."

After all the years of beating my head through different Walls, I started learning how to take more consistent Leaps of Faith. In this area, Nicole has been one of my master teachers. Being in relationship with her has brought up my deepest fears, particularly when we were dating. It was one *Yes Yes Hell No!* after another. It was a series of tough decisions to hang in there and see where the relationship went. And in the end, saying yes to Nicole is one of the best choices I've ever made.

Where Walls create pain and frustration, Leaps of Faith create freedom and joy. They do feel scary because they take you outside your comfort zone, but if you're willing to go there you'll also get to everywhere you most want to be.

Leaps of Faith are the surest indicators of the lessons you're here to learn. They're the compass needle pointing toward true north.

Then there's one more case to consider. The most confusing situation is when intuition says yes and reason says no. When this happens, you may be facing an extra-strength Leap of Faith which the voice of reason can't yet comprehend, and your opportunity is to take the leap. Or you may be on course, but your particular choices aren't as grounded as they could be and your opportunity is to explore more effective ways to move forward. Or, as a third possibility, you might be misunderstanding the voice of intuition, and the choice you're considering might involve a real and present danger.

When this conflict happens, slow down. Reach out for support. Breathe. Get help. Meditate. Journal. Pause.

Don't worry. Clarity will come, along with great gifts.

Happiness. Success. Growth. Love. Connection.

And even the meaning of life.

In today's day and age, some of the most challenging and important questions are those involving meaning and purpose. What are you meant to do? What is your purpose? Does your life have meaning? If so, what is it going to be?

Answering these questions requires taking a step back and looking at the bigger picture. So let's do that, by taking a look at who we really are, and why we're really here.

Chapter 11

The Meaning of Life

"We're on this planet for too short a time. And at the end of the day, what's more important? Knowing that a few meaningless figures balanced – or knowing that you were the person you wanted to be?" ~ Sophie Kinsella

Human beings are more than just a bag of bones and blood. The religious traditions may disagree on the exact nature of the soul or spirit that animates the body. They may differ on the details of what happens to us after we die. But they're unanimous in their proclamation of a great truth:

Who we are, at our core, is greater than we can imagine.

Call it heart, soul, spirit, love – we are not just human beings. As Theilard de Chardin put it,

"We are spiritual beings having a human experience."

Who you are, at your core, is Love. It's not something you need to prove yourself worthy of, and it's not something you can achieve.

It's who you Are. And the purpose of life is to Remember.

Now that's a rather bold claim, and not everyone will agree with it. So let's focus on what we can agree on.

Let's say that as human beings we're made up of three parts: *body*, *mind*, and *spirit*. These are the three selves. And while there are a host of voices scattered between these selves, the primary voice of the body is the voice of *fear*.

The Three Selves

Intuition
(Yes)

Reason
(Yes)

Fear
(Hell No!)

Spirit
(Fulfillment)

Mind
(Success)

Body
(Survival)

The primary voice of the mind is that of *reason*. And the primary voice of the spirit is that of *intuition*.

Each of these three aspects has its own set of needs. The body's needs are all about *survival* – sex, hunger, safety, and shelter. The mind's needs are all about *success* – approval, achievement, fame, and fortune. The spirit's needs are all about *fulfillment* – growth, contribution, connection, and creativity.

We experience fulfillment when we do something meaningful. When we have a wave of personal and spiritual growth, that's fulfilling. When we give to others or make a difference in someone's life, that's fulfilling. When we create connection from a place of love and caring, that's fulfilling. And when we participate in the act of creation, in any realm of life – art, business, science, or family, that's fulfilling.

If we were to talk to a thousand people on their deathbeds and ask what mattered most to them in their lives, we'd hear a thousand stories about these same four things.

These are the needs of the soul. Fulfilling these needs is the meaning of life.

The meaning of life is growth, contribution, connection, and creativity.

When we're on purpose, the voice of intuition lights up. We feel a sense of joy and inspiration and we develop in consciousness. We increase in our awareness of our true, loving, spiritual self. At the same time, waking up is scary. It triggers our deepest fears. That's why one of the surest guides to finding your purpose is to look for your *Yes Yes Hell No!*

Almost everyone wants to find their purpose in life, yet most people misunderstand how this concept of purpose works. In some form, most people keep looking for "The One" – that one special career, activity, or relationship that they were put here to take part in. As I wanted when I was dating Nicole, they want to be told, "This is it. This is your purpose. Go do this one thing and you'll be safe, successful, and fulfilled."

But that's not how it works.

There are millions of ways your purpose can show up. If something involves growth, contribution, connection, or creativity – you're on purpose. Some things will light up brighter than others: there are definitely areas where your calling will be stronger than others, and your purpose can change directions at any time, but there isn't any one thing that you were meant to do.

While my years in Silicon Valley were filled with insecurity, they were also filled with an incredible sense of purpose. I was at ground zero of the Internet Revolution, doing my part to help change the world. Plus, I had a deep connection to the people I was working with, I got to create a new business from scratch, and I grew more in those eight years than I would have thought possible.

But with the second burnout, my passion disappeared. One day it was there, and the next day it was gone. It was like I was swimming in a fast moving river, and then it suddenly dried up.

When this happened, my voice of fear wanted me to keep going, find an even more impressive job, and make an even bigger pile of money. But my voice of intuition knew it was time for a change.

I'd like to say that it was an easy transition, but it took a year of being mired in depression for me to admit I was in crisis, that things were only getting worse, and that I needed to reach out for help.

In desperation, I started opening up about my problems and a friend suggested that I try a five day self-awareness seminar called Insight. Something about her description of the program both inspired and scared me. I was both drawn to this workshop, and freaked out by it. It was a clear *Yes Yes Hell No!*

So I signed up. I showed up. And that one, little, on-course decision changed my life in profound ways.

As a three year old child, my pain was so large and my coping skills so small that when my mother died, I didn't know how to grieve her death. After my father remarried and I had a new mother, I did my best to move on with my new life. But there was still this big ball of pain inside me. So my voice of fear stepped in, buried the wound, and locked it away. I repressed it so thoroughly that I didn't even know it was there.

As a young adult when people would ask me about my birth mother, I'd tell them that she died when I was so young that I didn't even remember her. And it felt like my truth. But it wasn't. In reality, the pain wasn't gone. It was waiting.

While repression feels like a pain-removal device, it stores pain until we're ready to heal it.

On the last day of this seminar, for the first time since childhood, I connected to the pain of my mother's death – the wound I'd been unconsciously running from all these years.

One moment I was an adult, and the next moment I'd regressed to being a three year old child, clutching my chest and crying "Mommy, mommy! Ow! Ow! Ow! Don't go! Don't GOOOO!!!"

For the first time in twenty-seven years, I connected with the pain of my mother's death, and I was able to start grieving her loss. I spent the day connecting with Little Brian and his sadness. I grieved. And as I did so, a miracle happened. I moved through my deepest pain and fear, and had a taste of the love on the other side.

For years I'd been seeking love "out there." But on that day, everything changed. Suddenly I *knew,* not as a concept but as a reality, that beneath all my fears who I am is love. Infinite, indescribable love.

I discovered that what I'd most been seeking was already inside. I met my soul. I had a taste of Reality.

For an over-achieving, arrogant agnostic, let's just say that this came as a bit of a shock.

It took another year, and a handful of similar experiences, for me to walk away from a ridiculously lucrative career and immerse myself in a full time journey of healing and growth. It was terrifying, but it was what I needed to do.

I now knew, in a way I couldn't argue with, that until I healed this wound I couldn't have the relationship I craved – either with myself, with Spirit, or with my future wife and family.

My soul's path took a turn. It took a lot – a Wall, a Leap of Faith and a miracle – for me turn with it. And thank God I did.

In talking about words like God, soul and Spirit, I'm less interested in talking about religion than in spirituality. In my experience, *spirituality* is synonymous with *meaning.* If something is truly spiritual, it has meaning. And if something has meaning, it's spiritual. It's on our soul's path.

All the great religions are rooted in spirituality. It forms their common core. And they cover a lot of other territory as well: theology, morality, tradition, hierarchy, ritual, power, pride – there's a lot that can get wrapped up in the quest for the divine.

For me, religion is like a stained-glass window, filled with patterns and pictures. Spirituality is the light that makes the window shine. Both are beautiful and important.

Spirituality doesn't cause conflict. It's based on experiences (such as growth, contribution, connection and creativity) upon which we can all agree.

At the same time, spirituality is scary. It challenges us to embrace growth at our deepest levels of being. It takes us far beyond our comfort zone. It requires taking regular Leaps of Faith.

Spirituality – which is at the heart of all religion as well as the heart of all of life – is about action more than belief. It's about courage more than comfort. And ultimately, it's about the practice of leaping and being caught.

Chapter 12

The Practice of Leaping and Being Caught

"Faith is taking the first step even when you don't see the whole staircase." ~ Martin Luther King Jr.

aith has been one of the most challenging topics in my life. I was raised in a devoutly religious family. As an intellectual teenager, I began to question the beliefs I'd been raised with and found that I couldn't reconcile them with my scientific worldview. So when I moved out to go to college, I also moved away from my family's church and became an atheist.

This lasted for a year or two, until a friend of mine pointed out that it takes just as much faith to believe there isn't a God as to believe that there is.

Boy, did that ever mess with my head.

Thankfully, there was a way out. I became a devout agnostic. I declared the whole question out of bounds. I decided to worship at the altar of achievement instead.

Oh, and did I mention the burnouts that followed?

It would be another ten years before I found a definition of faith that worked for me, because I thought that faith was primarily about group-based beliefs. To me, it was about religion, about righteousness, about belonging.

The problem was that everyone seemed to disagree. How could one group be right and everyone else be wrong? How could truth create so many wars and conflict?

What I didn't realize is that there are two types of faith – belief-based faith and action-based faith – and that they work in very different ways.

Belief-based faith is something you *have*: "I have faith that our beliefs are true." Action-based faith is something you *do*: "I am taking a Leap of Faith."

Belief-based faith is rooted in ideas. Its purpose is to help you understand. "I have faith in the power of love and forgiveness." Action-based faith is rooted in practice. Its purpose is to help you grow. "I am taking a Leap of Faith which both excites and scares me."

Belief-based faith can provide comfort, clarity, courage, and connection. However, it can also create conflict. Have you noticed that the more important your beliefs are to you, the more defensive you tend to get when they're attacked or questioned? You may even be bothered when others don't share them.

When you're in fear, you need to be right about your beliefs. And the more important your beliefs, the stronger your fears become when those beliefs are questioned.

This doesn't just apply to religious beliefs: it applies to all beliefs. In family life, this pattern creates conflict over the right way to raise children. In politics, it creates conflict over the right way to govern. In academia, it creates conflict over the right theories and paradigms. This is why Max Planck said that "Science advances one funeral at a time."

At the end of the day, all beliefs require a certain amount of faith. And belief-based faith is extremely important. It's just not the subject of this book.

Action-based faith – the practice of taking actions that cause you to grow – is the whole point of this book.

For action-based faith is nothing less than the practice of discovering the places where your spirit says, "Go forward" and your fear says, "Go back." It's the practice of gathering your courage and saying yes in the face of your fears. It's about living your purpose and walking your path. It's about leaping.

And, just as important, it's about being caught.

In the domain of action, faith is the practice of leaping and being caught.

Leaps of Faith are profoundly self-honoring acts. They're among the most intelligent choices you can make.

The practice of leaping and being caught is the surest tool for making Big Decisions and creating Big Wins. It provides concrete, consistent, and compelling benefits, right here, right now.

After a long and crazy path, I am living in the last place I expected, married to the last woman I expected, doing the last thing I expected – and living a life that's better than I ever *could* have expected.

It's taken me quite a while, but after enough Leaps of Faith, I've learned to trust that my spirit is much better at this game than my mind is, and that both are much wiser than my fears.

Section II

HOW YOUR LIFE IMPROVES WITH EACH YES YES HELL NO!

Chapter 13

The Gift of Growth

"Life is change. Growth is optional. Choose wisely."
~ Karen Kaiser

L eaps of Faith come with powerful, practical benefits. In this section, we're going to explore ten of the most important gifts you can receive from using this tool, starting with the gift of personal and spiritual growth.

Like all living things, you're either growing or dying. Always. There is no other option. Stay too long in your comfort zone and you begin to die, slowly, a little bit each day.

Notice, in contrast, that when you're growing you feel alive and on purpose. Your life has meaning. Sure, you may feel scared at times, but you're also excited.

This isn't to say that you should always be pushing, or that it's not okay to relax and have fun. Growth works best when you alternate between periods of healthy challenges and periods of rest and rejuvenation. It's like working out at the gym. Weight training involves pushing the muscles hard, to the point where they start to break down, and then giving them 24 to 48 hours to recover and grow. Personal growth works best when you approach it in a similar way.

There are many ways to grow. Human beings can develop physically, as when babies learn to walk or adults increase their fitness levels. We can develop emotionally, as when children learn to share their toys or adults expand their ability to resolve conflicts. We can develop mentally, as when teenagers learn calculus or adults increase their time management skills. And we can develop spiritually, as when people create loving connections or make a difference in the lives of others.

Growth can also happen at different levels of depth. The most common form of growth involves developing new skills and *competencies*, such as learning how to master a new sport or computer program. At a deeper level, growth involves developing *character* – working on traits like honesty, loyalty, responsibility, and caring. At the deepest level, growth involves evolving in *consciousness* – the way you see and experience the world.

This core level of growth is both the most important and the least understood. More than anything else, your level of consciousness determines your experience of life – whether you feel happy or sad, whether you find relationships safe or scary, and whether you experience life in terms of abundance or scarcity.

It's possible to live at varying levels of consciousness. Think of a ladder of consciousness, with your position on that ladder determining your *experience* of life. How happy are you? What are you feeling? How are you being in the world each day? Are you living from a place of love and joy, or from a place of fear and judgment?

Your position on the ladder also determines your *perspective* – the place from which you view the world – and therefore what you can or can't see. As you look around, do you see lack or plenty? Do you perceive people as trustworthy or suspicious? Do you view things as getting better or worse? Are you looking at the big picture and all you have to be grateful for, or are you focused on all the little things that feel frustrating and scary?

At the top of this ladder is all that we most want in life: love, joy, inspiration, creativity, happiness, freedom, peace, trust, fulfillment, connection. At the bottom of this ladder are the things we least want: fear, pain, guilt, shame, anger, hatred, loneliness.

The voice of fear lives at the bottom of the ladder. This isn't to say that fear is bad or wrong: it's just painful. The voice of intuition lives at the top, and the voice of reason lives in the middle.

Think of a moment when you felt absolutely loved and connected. Consider the people you were with and the location you were in. What were you doing? Were you worried about the future, or were you present in the moment?

That's an example of what the world feels like when you're living from the top of the ladder of consciousness.

Now, think of something that scares you. Do you agonize over finances or worry about your children? Do you worry about not being good enough? Fearing rejection? Avoiding failure? Think of a fear and repeat it to yourself. Give it your awareness. Focus on it then notice what happens to your body. How do you feel? Does the world seem more or less safe?

You've just experienced a shift in consciousness.

I'm in a high state of consciousness when I put Annibelle to bed. I'll take her upstairs and she'll say, "I want to sleep in Mommy's bed." I'll ask her if she wants to go to sleep by herself, and she'll say "No. Cuddles!" So I'll ask her if she wants just a few cuddles. "No! Lots of cuddles!" I love everything about our routine – giving her a bottle while we snuggle and I read, brushing her teeth and afterwards having her fall asleep in my arms with a smile on her face.

Heaven.

In this place, the world is perfect. There's no scarcity or fear, and there's no need to fix or change anything. There's just love, connection, and abundance.

This is in sharp contrast to the contracted moments when my fears come up. "I'm scared I won't make enough money to take care of my family" "I'm afraid I'm going to lose their love" "I'm worried about all the work I have to do this week." When I give these fears energy, my consciousness drops, and I shift from abundance to scarcity. From this place I start worrying about my business, and wondering whether I can get enough clients this year. I start stressing about things that don't really need my attention.

Consciousness is more than just a state of mind. It's the place inside you're living from which determines how you're able to see and experience the world.

The voice of intuition speaks from the world of love and Spirit. In this place, there's no need for war, hatred, or fear. In this world of abundance, those things literally don't make sense.

The voice of fear speaks from the world of scarcity and loss. These are two separate worlds. And more than anything else – more than personality, accomplishments, skills, or even character – your level of consciousness determines the quality of your life.

Was there a recent time when you just "lost it?" Things were going fine then something flipped inside and your emotions took over? In the blink of an eye, you switched from being Dr. Jekyll to Mr. Hyde?

That's what it's like to change consciousness. It's a shift: not just in how you're feeling, but in whom you're being.

Are you serious about intentionally creating your life? Do you really want to turn your dreams into reality? If so, moving up the ladder of consciousness is the most powerful way to do so.

And *Yes Yes Hell No!* is your surest guide to getting there.

The voice of intuition lights up around decisions that would move you higher on the ladder of consciousness. That's its primary job and purpose.

The voice of fear screams out around decisions that would pull you out of your comfort zone. While anyone can change states in an instant, more permanent shifts up the ladder require deep growth and lasting change.

This level of growth and change – changing your life, your perspective, who you are – automatically triggers fear. It brings up a big "Hell No!" inside.

With their opposite reactions, the voices of intuition and fear indicate *what* your growth opportunities are. Then the voice of reason helps you ground your decisions as you seek to determine *how* to follow an opportunity in the easiest and most efficient ways possible.

Growing up, I had hundreds of so-called character-building experiences, many of which seemed to involve delivering newspapers at an ungodly hour on a Sunday morning in the middle of a Midwestern blizzard.

I remember – vividly – the time we turned on the radio and heard the news that the wind chill had dropped to fifty below zero.

Not just cold. Crazy cold. "We hope you make it back alive" cold.

Each time this happened, the voice of fear was pretty clear that it would be a *lot* more comfortable to stay home and go back to bed. "Should I go outside?" "Heck, no! Are you crazy?!" (I'm sure it would have said "Hell No!" except that my voice of fear was raised in a very polite household.)

Yet each time, another wiser, more mature voice inside told me to get out there and get the job done. And every time I did, I grew.

Your choices determine your character. Your character creates your level of consciousness. And your consciousness determines your destiny.

When you make your choices based on finding and acting on your *Yes Yes Hell No!* responses, you will build character and grow in consciousness. This is simple, but it's not necessarily easy. You'll need wisdom to discern one voice from the other, and you'll need courage and commitment to develop the practice of leaping and being caught.

You don't *have* to develop this practice. And, if you choose to do so, you'll discover just how powerful a tool it is for improving your life, because each step up the ladder of consciousness comes with a host of gifts, including the gift of connection.

Chapter 14

The Gift of Connection

"My friends tell me I have an intimacy problem. But they don't really know me." ~ Garry Shandling

In relationships, it's easy to let the voice of fear take control. With all the best intentions, you might end up listening to every "Hell No!" and treating it as truth. While you may equate closeness with feeling loved and happy, the reality is that the more you care about someone, the more vulnerable you are to being hurt.

The more you care about someone, the louder the voice of fear can become in that relationship.

While I care about my clients deeply, listening to them almost never triggers my fears. I'm able to hold a clean space for anything they want to share. Even if they get upset with me or challenge a direction I'm taking them in, I can be still and listen. But let my wife say something critical – or something I take as critical – and my voice of fear may just freak out. I sometimes get instantly defensive, wanting to pull away and do the opposite of what she's asking from me. Not because I don't care about her, but because I care so much.

Sometimes, when we're out for a drive, Nicole will suggest that I take a different route and I'll refuse. It's a silly little thing that wouldn't bother me if it came from anyone else. Yet from her, it's suddenly a problem.

When conflicts come up in relationships, they require us to make decisions, big or small. Do I take the route Nicole suggests, or do I refuse? Do I close my heart, or do I open it? Do I get angry and resist, or do I practice acceptance?

How a couple handles conflict is the number one predictor of long-term marital happiness. So over time, every little decision can become a really big deal.

The key to navigating these conflicts is to pull apart the three voices. Again, the real conflict isn't between different choices, it's between different voices. When emotions get triggered, it's not particularly accurate to say "I'm angry" or "I'm scared." It's more accurate to say "My voice of fear is upset" or "I'm aware that some fears are coming up for me." And that's not a bad thing.

Each and every aspect of each and every person is doing the best it knows how.

The voice of fear can show up as anger, insecurity, guilt, unworthiness, frustration, or even hatred. No matter how it presents itself, it always has a positive purpose. It's trying to keep you safe and help you get your needs met the best way it knows how.

There's no way around it. Relationships are scary. They pull you outside of your comfort zone. The closer you get to someone, and the more important someone becomes to you, the more dangerous a relationship can feel.

So how do you work with this?

By navigating with *Yes Yes Hell No!*

When I get thrown off by something Nicole says, I now know enough to recognize this as an opportunity for growth. I'm in that place where I've opened my heart to such a point that my fears are being triggered. If I check in with the voice of fear, and let it speak as fear – not as anger or judgment or defensiveness or anything else – it often says things like, "It's not safe to be so vulnerable" or "I'm scared she doesn't really love me."

If I then consistently check in with the voice of intuition, which is also the voice of mature love, I'm able to connect with just how much I care about my wife. And from that place, the voice of reason is usually able to find an easy way to resolve the issue.

In the case of the driving conflict, the voice of reason doesn't see it as any big deal. "Nicole's desire to be in control is just her voice of fear speaking. It's not her truth, and it doesn't mean that she doesn't love or respect me. So let's use this as an opportunity to practice connecting. If it makes her feel better if I take the other route, terrific! It's a chance to show her how much I care."

In relationships, each step to greater intimacy requires a Leap of Faith. So look for them and then take action.

Now this doesn't mean we should tolerate abuse, or that every relationship is a fit. Sometimes the most courageous *Yes Yes Hell No!* is the decision to leave a relationship after it's no longer serving you.

Notice how difficult a Leap of Faith can be to find when you're upset or stuck – when the voice of fear is running the show. Later, in chapter 32, we'll look at some tools for how to work with the three voices, particularly when things feel out of control.

For now, it's enough to recognize that *Yes Yes Hell No!* is the surest guide through the tricky terrain of relationship. It will get you out of the wrong ones, into the ones that truly nourish you, and through whatever conflicts and discord may arise. As your Leaps of Faith carry you into a more connected, more loving, more spacious version of yourself, you'll experience more of what you most want in every realm of life, including the gift of abundance.

Chapter 15

The Gift of Abundance

"Not what we have But what we enjoy, constitutes our abundance." ~ Epicurus

People often look to money for their happiness. But don't we all know people who are both rich and unhappy? If you don't, turn on the TV. There are plenty of them around and they seem to get a lot of airtime.

Some of the most meaningful and precious moments happen in situations where money is irrelevant, as when people are on their deathbeds.

When my grandmother died at the age of 83, I was sitting next to her, holding her hand. Our family was gathered around her and we had all taken time to share our love with her. As her breathing slowed and then stopped, she didn't seem scared or worried. She had lived a full and good life, and as she passed we were filled with a deep sense of peace. We cried a lot at her funeral, but our tears were filled with joy for her life as much as sadness for her passing.

True abundance is an *experience* of freedom, joy, trust, and well-being. It's that place where you're grateful for what you have, while also opening yourself to more. It can be *aided* by having wealth, but it can't be *created* by it. True abundance often includes the nicer things in life, but it's not dependent on them. They become the icing on the cake rather than the food needed for survival.

Wealth measures how much you have. Abundance is a state of being.

Think about it. If you had to pick one or the other, which would you choose? Having money or experiencing freedom? Having the approval of others or experiencing love?

I have the honor of calling Sean Stephenson my friend. Three feet tall, bound to a wheelchair, and with bones so brittle they sometimes break when he sneezes, Sean lives life larger than almost anyone I know. He is married to a beautiful, amazing woman, and he's one of the most powerful motivational speakers I've met. Who Sean *is* shines brighter than anything about his condition, and while I'm sure he'd prefer to have better health, his experience of life is happier and more abundant than that of most people I know.

This isn't to denigrate material success, or to say that it's not important. Money matters. So do health, approval, and accomplishments. But how often do you stop to ask "What matters more?" Success *can* help you improve your experience of life, but it can also be a distraction, a trap, and a prison.

One of the keys to making great decisions toward creating a great life is to distinguish between these two dimensions – the ladder of success and the ladder of consciousness.

The ladder of success measures your gains in life in terms of what you *have*. How much money do you have? How much beauty? Status? How many possessions?

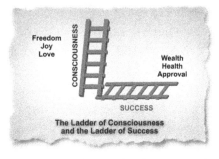

Freedom
Joy
Love

CONSCIOUSNESS

Wealth
Health
Approval

SUCCESS

The Ladder of Consciousness
and the Ladder of Success

Friends? Climbing this ladder results in health, wealth,

and approval. Failing to climb this ladder leads to poverty, sickness, and rejection.

The ladder of consciousness measures your *experience* in life. How happy are you? What are you feeling? How do you show up in the world each day? Are you living from a place of love and joy, or from a place of fear and judgment? Are you experiencing abundance or scarcity?

The ladder of success may be easy to measure, but it's difficult to trust. When you make it your compass, you never really know where you're going to end up.

In contrast, the ladder of consciousness is harder to measure, but easy to trust. No matter what happens, it points to true north. With every step up this ladder, your experience of life improves. Your capacity for love increases. And the meaning of your life expands.

Moving up the ladder of consciousness is moving into true abundance. It's a way of being in the world that's more fulfilling than collecting any number of shiny objects. This is not a theoretical ideal or a moral prescription, but a practical, fundamental tool for creating the life you most want.

How do you move up the ladder of consciousness? You find a *Yes Yes Hell No!* and turn it into a Leap of Faith, one decision at a time.

When people ask me how I came to this career. I sometimes joke that the problems all started the third time I became rich. My thirtieth birthday should have been cause for celebration. After years of hard work, our company had just gone public, and I was suddenly rich enough to retire. At thirty. Where the first two times I'd created millions on paper, this time my wealth looked real.

This freaked me out.

After years of climbing the ladder of success as hard and as fast as I could, I'd achieved almost everything I wanted. Yet inside I felt insecure and empty. And no matter how many women I dated, I still felt scared and alone.

Even worse, after years of climbing, I no longer knew which way to go. I could no longer pretend that by itself the ladder of success was going to get me where I wanted to be. I'd climbed high enough, early enough, that I could no longer fool myself about its real value. Yet I'd also left my family's religion behind for good, and so I no longer had a clear path to follow.

If their religion didn't work for me, and my striving for success didn't either, well how was I going to find the love and joy I craved? My inability to answer this question led to that year of depression, second burnout, and emotional crisis.

It took a lot for me to reach out for help and take a Leap of Faith, by signing up for that scary sounding seminar. But in doing so I had a direct experience of abundance. I went through a shift in consciousness, where I was able to see the two ladders for what they really were. I was given a taste of what life feels like at the top of the ladder of consciousness. And that inspired me to take my life in an entirely new direction.

A dozen years later, my life has become better than I could have imagined. I enjoy my successes, but I'm no longer addicted to them. I appreciate money, but it no longer defines my self-worth. I treasure relationships, but I'm no longer as dependent on the approval of others. And I have a career, a family, an entire life that I absolutely love.

All because I developed the practice of following *Yes Yes Hell No!* and getting the support I needed to do so. I learned how to consistently make great decisions, and in the process discovered something unexpected: the gift of flow.

Chapter 16

The Gift of Flow

"The moment one definitely commits oneself, then providence moves too. All sorts of things occur to help one that would never otherwise have occurred. A whole stream of events issues from the decision, raising in one's favor all manner of unforeseen incidents, meetings and material assistance which no man could have dreamed would have come his way. Whatever you can do or dream you can, begin it. Boldness has genius, power and magic in it. Begin it now." ~ *Johann Goethe*

All this talk of fear and faith can make this sound like a painful path. I'm with you! I was raised in a family whose motto was "If it's hard, give it to a Whetten." Now, this motto came with great gifts. It helped me develop courage, commitment, and the capacity for hard work. I'm a better person for it. But if you believe in the Law of Attraction and the truth that "where you focus is where you go," then it's also a bit like wearing a spiritual "kick me" sign. Ouch!

Now that I'm a parent, my wife and I are seeking a new motto. "If it involves growth and abundance, with as much grace and ease as possible, give it to a Whetten." I know. It doesn't have the same ring to it. We'll just call it a work in progress.

Growth can be hard for sure, but it doesn't have to be. And while Leaps of Faith can be scary, they can also be exciting. You'll notice quickly that the more you practice leaping and being caught, the more the universe conspires on your behalf. Striving gives way to ease. And one of the ways this shows up is through the experience of flow.

Think of a time when you were "in the zone." Perhaps you were exercising and your movements became effortless. Maybe you were doing something creative and the ideas just started pouring in. Or you were working on a project and with each next step you knew exactly what to do.

Flow. There's nothing like it.

When you're in flow, time flies by. Productivity skyrockets. You have remarkable focus, are completely present, and can create extraordinary results.

For me, writing is all about the dance between flow and no flow. There are times when I'm not in flow, and every word feels like a struggle. I get stuck in my head and it hurts. I'm blocked. I don't even like reading what I wrote.

But when I'm in flow, everything changes. Inspiration bubbles up. Creativity rushes in. What comes out of me feels pure and clear, sometimes brilliant. I find myself in a space of creation that's bigger than my mind and far larger than my fears.

Being in flow is one of my greatest joys. But the thing about flow is you can't control it. You can't just turn it on.

While you can access stress anytime, you can't force your way to flow.

At the same time, flow doesn't appear at random. It's not something that just happens to you. It certainly doesn't just happen to special people.

Flow is a direct result of making decisions that raise your level of consciousness. Flow shows up when you live in alignment with your purpose and path.

	Intuition	Reason	Fear
Tiger	No	No	**Hell No!**
Wall	No	Yes	
Leap of Faith	Yes	Yes	
Flow	**Yes**	**Yes**	**Yes**

One decision at a time, the more often you step into a *Yes Yes Hell No!*, the less life scares you and the more you get to live in flow.

There are two sides to flow – an inner experience and an outer reality. The inner experience is one of "being in the zone" – what Gay Hendricks calls our "zone of genius." This is when what we do feels easy and graceful yet has tremendous value.

The outer aspect of flow shows up as synchronicity – those magical moments when the universe drops its mask of neutrality, gives you a wink, and clearly shows how it's conspiring in your favor.

Synchronicity is one of the surest signs of being on purpose.

Flow is both a reward and a confirmation. You find yourself in a state of grace, swimming with the river instead of fighting against it. This is on-course feedback from the universe, one of the ways that you're caught on the other side of a Leap of Faith. Flow is what happens when you've committed to a *Yes Yes Hell No!* and then you Make Friends With Your Fears (which I talk more about in chapter 32) to get them to drop away. You land in Yes Yes Yes! – all three voices are aligned. You might experience this as excitement, inspiration, synchronicity, laughter, or peace. Flow is truly a gift.

And it's a great reason for gratitude.

Chapter 17

The Gift of Gratitude

"If the only prayer you said was thank you, that would be enough." ~ Meister Eckhart

Human beings have a remarkable ability to focus on the negative. Consider these facts. Over the past one hundred years the average U.S. life expectancy has increased by 52 percent. Infant mortality has decreased by 92 percent. Real per-person income has increased by 420 percent. And there's now more computing power in a single mobile phone than the entire country used to have.

The United States has become a country where we *drive* to our protests.

While my grandparents worried about whether they could feed their children at all, I worry about the dangers of feeding our daughters non-organic blueberries.

The reality is that we live in one of the most advanced, abundant, and peaceful times in history.

Yet many people are miserable.

Furthermore, we seem to thrive on negativity. Studies show that up to 94 percent of news articles are negative. 72 percent of Americans think our nation's morals are getting worse. And despite a sharp drop in violent crime over the past decade, 68 percent of people think there's more crime than a year ago.

As Louis C.K. says, "Everything's amazing but nobody's happy."

We all have things we *could* be grateful for. And we may have things we think we *should* be grateful for. Yet for most people, most of the time, the actual experience of gratitude eludes us. We live in fear and negativity instead.

Fear isn't wrong, but it is addictive. The more we focus on the negative, the worse we feel, and the worse we feel, the more we feel compelled to search for what's wrong.

Where you focus is where you go. Given half a chance, the voice of "Hell No!" can easily take over the show.

As strange as it may sound, a big part of the problem is that we no longer have that many things to be genuinely frightened of in our life. It's becoming ever harder for the voice of fear to do its real job, and so it tends to create unproductive "make-work" instead. Having no real and present dangers to respond to, it obsesses over little, niggly, or even imaginary issues.

The voice of fear is anchored in our reptilian brain. It's a hardwired response that's evolved over millions of years, and it has the capacity to provide us with intense bursts of energy.

Living in the wild, an animal will see a predator, go into fight or flight mode, escape the danger and then rest. When we're responding to real and present dangers, such as a speeding car or a mountain lion, the voice of fear turns on, gives the body extra energy to get through the crisis, and then turns off.

However, there just aren't that many real Tigers for us to face anymore. Instead, we create endless little things to worry about. "Were we overcharged for our car repairs?" "Am I answering enough of my emails?" "Are the kids eating enough greens?" "Do I look fat in this outfit?"

Without those occasional big Tigers to deal with, we seem to come up with a million mirages to get alarmed about instead. And since these fears are primarily self-generated, there's nothing we can do "out there" to make them go away. We can never run fast enough to get off this particular treadmill.

In contrast, gratitude serves us well. It's both a gift and a practice. And along with growth and genuine service, it's one of the most effective tools for making the shift to a higher level of consciousness, from scarcity to abundance.

Up to this point, this book has mostly focused on how to make concrete, external, Big Decisions: "Do I want to get married?" "Should I take this new job?" Yet this tool can be even more valuable when you apply it internally.

The voice of fear screams of danger. The voice of intuition sings with gratitude. If there's a genuine Tiger, run. That's a fear that's worth listening to. Otherwise your opportunity in meeting your fears each

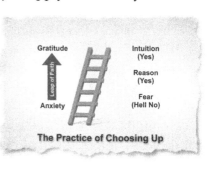

day is to practice taking little internal Leaps of Faith, one at a time. Instead of focusing on the negative, focus on the positive. Instead of choosing stress, practice gratitude. Instead of feeding your fears, look for all that feeds and supports you.

When faced with a choice between love and fear, between acceptance and judgment, or between gratitude and anxiety – choose up.

Even turning on the news involves a choice. Will you give in to the voice of fear and heap even more concerns on your pile of worries? That's one option. Another option is to pause, take a breath, and ask yourself, "Is this a real and present danger to me or my loved ones, right here and right now?" If the answer is yes, go to, "Is there some immediate action I can take to address the problem?"

If the answer is no, then it's an opportunity not to get upset and worried, but to choose up instead. It's an opportunity to take a stand for what's good in the world rather than to dive into the sea of negativity.

This may sound simple, or even trivial – far from it. It takes strength to face your fears and redirect your energies. It takes acceptance to listen to negativity without either feeding it or fighting it, without making it right or making it wrong. And it takes faith to reach for the light when you feel surrounded by darkness.

The practice of gratitude is its own little miracle. It's both a choice and a consequence. It's both the risk and the reward. It's both the action of leaping and the gift of being caught.

Gratitude is foreign to the voice of fear. It's a program that doesn't compute. "If I stop being afraid, then I won't have any power." "If I'm grateful, then I'll stop growing. "If I focus on the positive, then I'm being irresponsible." "If I let go of my fear, then I won't be able to make a difference."

From a place of abundance, these statements sound ridiculous. It's just obvious that wallowing in negativity makes everything worse. But when you're in a place of scarcity, fearful thoughts sound like truth. To the voice of fear, only fear makes sense.

Again, fear isn't wrong, just addictive. And it can't just be dismissed no matter how hard you try. Have you ever tried to tell your fears to shut up and go away? At least for me, that only seems to make them worse. Fears don't respond very well to being told that they're wrong. What they do respond to is a combination of acceptance and strength.

If you want your fears to let up, the first step is to listen to them from a place of acceptance and love. Then take actions to move through them, from a place of strength and courage. As you do so, you'll find your fears dropping away, and in their place you'll find a space appearing which you can fill with gratitude instead.

Leilanna is our joy baby. She has so much enthusiasm for life that she can barely contain it. Literally. When she was eight months old, she'd sometimes start laughing so hard that she'd lose muscle control and start thrashing around on the couch. While giggling. It was like a joy seizure.

In contrast, my email inbox seems like a perpetual war that I keep losing. This stresses me out. It triggers my fears of failure, unworthiness, and more. It's like all those emails are just sitting there, taunting me, telling me that I should have responded to them days ago. When this happens, my default response is to push harder – to focus on the negative, increase my stress, and try to use this to amp up and plow through them all. Yet this rarely works.

Thankfully, I've got a joy baby in the house who reminds me of how silly my fears can be. So I'm learning to breathe, acknowledge my fears, and just be with them. Then as they start to release, I shift my focus to the many, many things I have to be grateful for.

And suddenly, that overfull inbox just doesn't upset me the way it did before.

I invite you to turn this into a practice: love your fears, focus on the positive, take a leap, connect to some of the many things you have to be grateful for – and watch for the shift.

When we actually make the shift into gratitude and choose up in consciousness, we discover that love is more powerful than fear.

As we develop a practice of gratitude, we get to experience how acceptance can be the first step in creating lasting change. This opens the possibility of making an even bigger difference in the world as we develop the gifts of service and authentic leadership.

Chapter 18

The Gift of Service

"I slept and dreamt that life was joy. I awoke and saw that life was service. I acted and behold, service was joy." ~ Rabindranath Tagore

Genuine service feels delightful. There's nothing quite like the feeling that comes from making a difference in someone else's life.

As a new parent, I love helping our daughters learn. And I take great joy in how they enjoy it, too. "I'm not a baby, I'm a big girl!" "Again, again!" "I'm going to grow up super, super big!" "One more book!"

Books and bubbles, porcupines and poop – whatever the topic, they love learning, and I love being the one they listen to.

Yet there are also times when I'm fried, and no, I don't want to read one more book. I'd rather derail the *Little Train That Could* then go screaming through the night to *Where the Wild Things Are*. There are times when this nagging voice in my head says I should be doing more, and I just really don't want to. Sometimes I want to say no – to my children, friends, family, and clients – but I fear that doing so would make me selfish, unworthy, or irresponsible.

I was raised with stern expectations that I should be of service to others, and that any focus on myself (or even excessive self-care) could only be called selfish. Yet I've found that when I try too hard to be good, when I fall into over-giving, I find myself feeling tired, grumpy, and resentful.

This was a major challenge for me until I discovered the crucial distinction between *service* and *self-sacrifice*. True service is a Win/Win for everyone involved. It creates a cycle of giving and receiving that nourishes both parties.

While there's something inspiring about the *willingness* to sacrifice our needs for someone else, the regular *practice* of self-sacrifice is just not sustainable. If we equate self-care with selfishness, and consistently put others needs ahead of our own, it can only leave us feeling drained and empty with nothing left to give.

As a recovering overachiever, I still occasionally take on more than I can handle. When this happens, I get stressed out. My level of consciousness drops down a few notches, and my self-care goes out the window. I become less effective and that puts me even further behind. And pretty soon even the activities I most love, such as talking with my wife or dancing around with our daughters and singing *Who Let the Dogs Out*, just feel like painful, exhausting chores.

Nicole calls it my "pushy-pushies" – I call it the voice of fear. "I should be making more money." "I should be serving more clients." "I should be doing more to care for the children." "I should, I should, I should…"

When I let my fears take over and I commit to more things than I can handle, my magnificent life starts to feel miserable. I shift from gratitude to grumpiness, and I take out my frustrations on the people I love. I'll pull away from Nicole or lose my patience with our daughters. I become a much less enjoyable person to be around.

When we give from our overflow, service is a joy. When we're living from a consciousness of abundance, the most self-affirming thing we can do is give to others, and the most selfless thing we can do is take care of our own needs.

Yet when we over-commit and over-give, listening to the voice of fear and its many "shoulds," our so-called service only drains and depletes us. We end up killing any joy it might contain.

This doesn't mean that it's a problem when service feels challenging or pushes us beyond our comfort zone. Nicole had two difficult pregnancies, and her first months of

Service vs. Sacrifice

breastfeeding were both beautiful and brutal. It took a lot out of her and it often felt like a sacrifice. Her willingness to do whatever it took for our babies' well-being was a profound act of love.

At the same time, we were clear that her self-sacrifice was a conscious, short-term choice, and we made it a priority to help her get out of overstress as quickly and gracefully as possible. For the highest good of all concerned, Nicole chose to take care of her needs so she could get back to a place of abundance and true service.

This distinction isn't just a concept. And it's not just about having a positive attitude. It's the difference between two very different places in consciousness that we can live from.

When we're living from a place of fear and stress, or when we're not getting our own needs met, we see the world through the eyes of scarcity. There's not enough to go around and danger lurks behind every turn.

From this place, we have three choices for relationships: Win/Lose, Lose/Win or Lose/Lose. We can choose selfishness (I win and you lose), or self-sacrifice (I lose and you win). If neither of these works, then we end up with war, with both sides losing in order to keep the other from winning.

As we take care of our own needs, move up in consciousness, and shift to living from our heart and soul instead of from our fears and insecurities, our worldview changes. Instead of seeing a world ruled by scarcity, we see a world filled with abundance. Instead of needing to duke it out between winners and losers, we're able to create Win/Win relationships instead.

Playing Win/Win can be a challenge in certain relationships. It doesn't really work when the other person is playing Win/Lose, when we're trying to commit to more than we can handle, or when a Win/Win isn't even possible. In this case, if we try to force a Win/Win, we end up with a Lose/Win, back in self-sacrifice again.

Because of this, the highest form of relationship isn't Win/Win. It's Win/Win or No Deal. This means holding a total commitment to finding relationships that work for all concerned and to saying no to relationships that aren't a fit.

When our first daughter was born, we suddenly found ourselves overcommitted and overstressed. Who knew that a tiny baby could be so much work? Between friends, family, self-care, and careers, Nicole and I were both overcommitted well before Annibelle was born. Afterward, it felt like we were drowning. We had to figure out what to say no to – and fast.

On Nicole's side, a number of friendships suddenly weren't so Win/Win. She tends to feel more comfortable giving support than receiving it, and some of her friends (not to mention her husband), had gotten used to calling on her whenever they wanted to get help with their problems.

With Annibelle on the scene, Nicole needed to receive support rather than just give it. Intellectually, she understood this shift, but even the idea of saying no brought up some deep fears for her.

She wanted to nurture her baby, meet everyone else's needs, and take care of herself. But she couldn't do all that: something had to give. It wasn't easy, but she started saying no to her friends. She started saying no to me. Rather than buy into the fear-based belief that she should be able to do it all, she chose to prioritize herself and her baby. It was time to fill her cup back up. While this choice felt more selfish than self-affirming to her at the time, it was pivotal to Nicole's growth. It also upheld her ongoing commitment to being of genuine service in the world, as eventually her self-care restored her to a place of having more to give.

Bottom line, she had to either say no to some of her commitments, or say no to her growth in consciousness. Thankfully she managed to say no to the former more than the latter.

When life gets too full, we either have to reduce our commitments or else reduce our consciousness.

Holding for Win/Win or No Deal is both scary and safe. It's exciting and frightening. It requires courage because it means saying no to any number of "shoulds" that the mind suggests, but that aren't actually in the highest good.

Win/Win or No Deal always honors everyone's needs, but it rarely meets everyone's expectations.

Win/Win or No Deal requires learning how to prioritize our values, how to hold strong boundaries, and how to say no as an act of love. It involves choosing what's in the highest good instead of just going for what's popular. It's the key to living a life of genuine service, where we're experiencing the joy of contribution.

But it's not necessarily easy, because most of us have been trained that it's better to say yes than to say no.

It's just as important to learn how to say no as it is to say yes. Spoken with integrity, "no" is one of the most loving words we can say.

The truth is that we can only play Win/Win to the level that we're also able to play No Deal. So how do we develop this way of being in the world?

You guessed it: by looking for and acting on *Yes Yes Hell No!*

In this case, a "Hell No!" might show up as feelings of stress or a fear of saying no. The voice of fear may be worried about being rejected, feeling unworthy, or failing to live up to other people's expectations.

In times of overstress, the voice of intuition is an advocate for increased self-love, or self-affirming choices. It lights up around things that simplify our lives, that reduces expectations, that supports our self-care, and that allows us to slow down. It's a big fan of breathing. Stopping to smell the roses. Little kisses. Big hugs.

Then the voice of reason is responsible for ordering priorities and figuring out what to say no to. We connect to this voice by considering our highest values, by sorting through relationships with the criterion of Win/Win or No Deal, by dropping our "shoulds" and focusing on what's for the highest good of all concerned – including ourselves.

Again, this isn't about mastering an idea or a concept. It's a practice and a skill, like turning time management into a martial art.

Annibelle's birth brought up some hard choices for me as well. My voice of fear kept telling me about all the things I should still be doing, such as keeping up with friends, responding to all my emails, going to the gym, and running two different businesses. Obviously, I was striving for the impossible. I could certainly try to keep meeting my own overblown expectations and everyone else's to boot, but only at great cost.

My voice of intuition told me to trust. To have faith in our finances. To accept that I was overcommitted. To focus more on being than doing.

Then my voice of reason helped me create a priority list.
1.   Feed, diaper, and love the baby
2.   Take care of our basic needs (I mean *basic*, like sleep)
3.   Everything else

So I put one of my companies on ice, let my friends know that I was in a baby cave, stopped responding to ninety percent of my emails, and cut back on my exercise regime. For 18 months, I made a lot less money than I could have. The number of people I connected to was significantly smaller than I wanted to and was used to. But those relationships I did keep up with felt like a true Win/ Win. I was able to be present with our new baby, support and stay close to Nicole, take care of my needs, and provide exceptional value to my clients.

Does that sound simple? For me, it took a lot of courage. Like Nicole, I had to let some friendships fall away. I also released some goals that had been very dear to me.

Saying no can be scary. Yet as you do, you'll find that more and more of your life feels like an opportunity for genuine service, in which you're both giving and receiving, and truly living from a place of abundance.

Any number of gifts can come from living in alignment with genuine service, including the gift of authentic leadership.

Chapter 19

The Gift of Authentic Leadership

"There is a vacuum of competence that must be filled. Spiritually evolved people, by virtue of their discipline, mastery and love, are people of extraordinary competence, and in their competence they are called to serve the world, and in their love they answer the call." ~ M. Scott Peck

During my twenties, I thought leadership was all about me.

And for a while, it was.

As a twenty-six-year-old Berkeley student, I had the audacity to believe I could start a company, raise millions of dollars for it, and make it successful.

Looking back, I must have been insane.

I'm not sure how, but I managed to convince some serious venture capitalists (professional adults, who really should have known better) to invest millions of dollars in my dream. In doing so, I promptly discovered just how far I was over my head. I had no business experience, I'd never held a full-time job, and I didn't even know what I didn't know. I was in serious trouble. I was also committed. Fully. So I worked as hard as I could – 90 hours a week, every week, for four years.

One week we'd be on the edge of phenomenal success, and the next week we'd be on the brink of failure. This pattern repeated itself, through three rounds of funding, two strategic partnerships, and four failed attempts to replace myself as the CEO.

It was quite the ride.

When the company crashed and burned, I took the loss very personally. I'd made a lot of promises to a lot of people – investors, employees, customers – and I felt that I'd failed them all. It wasn't just that the company had failed. I had failed.

Because, of course, it was all about me.

I had more success with the acquiring company. After taking a few months off to recover, I moved into a position in which I had influence without responsibility, and a reasonable work load. I was told not to waste my time on investors, and then I snuck out and raised $10 million anyway.

It was like bringing home a puppy. "Look what I found! Can we keep it?"

I helped define our strategy, evangelize our products, and close some big customers. I flew around the world speaking, making liberal use of my expense account. I even helped the company raise another $60 million as part of a $400 million IPO.

It was still all about me.

My achievements. My responsibilities. The number of people I was managing. The money I had raised. The company gains that could be traced back to me. Leadership was about one thing – me.

Thankfully, the CEO of the acquiring company was a lot older and wiser, and one day he sat me down for a performance review. I don't remember the exact words, but it basically went like this.

"Brian, you're smart. We are so impressed with how smart you are. You are really, really smart. In fact, most of the time, you're the smartest person in the room. We love how smart you are. AND, you would be so much more effective if you could learn how to at least occasionally listen to what other people have to say."

His feedback brought me up short. Ouch. I'd been treating leadership as something I *do to* people rather than *do with* them. I'd been equating leadership with "being the hero" – always having the right answers, being the smartest person, putting in the most hours. And for the first time, I wondered if there might be a more effective way.

As an executive coach, I've encountered any number of leaders who think that leadership is all about them. It's their job is to be the hero, to be in control,

Heroic vs. Authentic Leadership

and to make everything work out. "How good am I?" "Do I know enough?" "Am I making enough money?" "How can I come up with the right strategy?" "Am I making the right decisions?" "Do people respect me?" "Do I have enough power?" These are typical questions Heroic Leaders ask.

In contrast, Authentic Leaders focus on the purposes they support and the people they serve. This isn't to say that they're martyrs, that they're weak, or that they're never thinking of themselves. Authentic Leaders build strong relationships that work for everyone. They build relationships based on Win/Win or No Deal.

This requires a great deal of courage and self-discipline. In a time of brutal competition and blistering change, Win/Lose thinking is almost automatic. "It's a dog-eat-dog world out there." "We need to beat our competitors and take their market share." "Business is war!"

From this perspective, Heroic Leadership just seems to make sense – life is a battle for survival and self-importance, and stress is the automatic price of success.

This wouldn't be so bad except that heroes are always supposed to be able to conquer their fears. They're taught to have the courage to conquer (which starts with determination), but not the courage to change (which starts with acceptance).

Acceptance is the foundation of lasting change. Yet this is the last thing that Heroic Leaders are trained to do.

These days, conquering the competition is much less important than keeping up with the exponential pace of change.

If you're a business leader and you're not alarmed by how fast things are changing, you're not paying attention. It's become the primary challenge of leadership. And Heroic Leadership is the opposite of what's required to deal with it.

Authentic Leaders are in the business of change. And that means playing a completely different game.

The job of a Heroic Leader is to have the right answers. The job of an Authentic Leader is to ask the right questions. Heroic Leaders worry about their level of importance. Authentic Leaders focus on their level of contribution. Heroic Leaders think life is a battle. Authentic Leaders live in a world of Win/Win or No Deal.

Heroic Leaders treat everything like a Tiger.

Authentic Leaders know the difference between Tigers and Walls, and they know when to take Leaps of Faith. They're masters of flow. They know when to conquer and when to change.

And they tend to be extraordinarily effective.

James Burke was the chairman of Johnson & Johnson in 1982, when seven people died from taking Tylenol capsules that had been pulled off the shelf of a Chicago store, replaced with cyanide, resealed, and put back for someone to buy. Suddenly, his company's products were being blamed for people's deaths, though the actual cause was entirely outside of his control. Burke could easily have gone on television and blamed the unknown criminal. He could have limited the recall to Chicago. He could have treated the problem as a Tiger, surrounded himself with lawyers, and done everything he could to protect his company's short term profits.

But he didn't respond that way at all.

Burke didn't assume he had the right answers. And he didn't jump to attack. Instead, he pulled together a seven-person strategy team and asked them to answer two questions. First, "How do we protect the people?" And second, "How do we save the product?"

As a result, the company instructed the nation to stop consuming the product, pulled every bottle of Tylenol from every store in the country, and issued a recall that cost them $100 million. They created triple-safety packaging, communicated their actions, and then re-released the product once they trusted it was safe.

Because of this, the company took a short term hit and created a long term success. They were able to both protect their customers and save a $350 million-per-year product. What could have been the end of their good name established their brand as supremely trustworthy. They turned an existential crisis into a Win/Win.

That's the power of Authentic Leadership.

Think of a leader who truly inspires you. Martin Luther King, Jr. Abraham Lincoln. Hillary Clinton. Nelson Mandela. Pope Francis.

These are strong, courageous and great leaders. Not because they were born with some special gene for leadership, but because they learned how to make leadership be about something much larger than themselves.

Authentic Leadership may sound naïve, idealistic, or unreachable. Not so. It's one of the most powerful forces on earth, and it's something anyone can develop. Walking the journey of Authentic Leadership can be complicated, but finding the path is simple. It merely requires a reliable guidance system – the ability to find and follow your *Yes, Yes, Hell No's*.

Chapter 20

The Gift of Authentic Success

"All I ask is the chance to prove that money can't make me happy." ~ Spike Milligan

The gifts we've talked about so far are all wonderful things. But what about money? Fame and fortune? Climbing the corporate ladder? How do these things fit into the equation? I don't know about you, but I really enjoy the finer things in life. I love five-star vacations. I love the feeling of knowing that my family's needs are taken care of. I love buying electronics, gifts for my wife, and nice cars.

Plus, I want a big, new beautiful home in L.A. for our family. With a huge backyard. On the beach.

Or at least within close driving distance.

So, here's the good news. You can absolutely have your cake and eat it too. You can absolutely create both money and meaning. You can absolutely experience both abundance and

Authentic vs. Stress Based Success

success. The key is to make sure that your successes are aligned with your purpose, rather than detracting from it.

It's learning to set goals that move you forward on your path, rather than away from it.

From a spiritual perspective, growth, contribution, connection, and creativity are required elements of life. Success is optional. You can create a purpose filled life that includes lots of success, or one that includes just a little. To your spirit, it doesn't really matter. It's like picking a flavor of ice cream. Which is better? Chocolate or vanilla? It depends on which you prefer.

What matters most is not how *big* a goal is, but how *aligned* it is.

As we learned in chapter 8, the best Big Wins are heartfelt, specific and scary. They're a *Yes Yes Hell No!* type of deal. And achieving them requires finding and taking regular Leaps of Faith.

Authentic success comes from committing to goals that are heartfelt, specific, and scary.

In contrast, many goals are rational, but uninspiring. They feel like a "should" or a "have to" instead of a true, exciting "want to." And when you pursue them, you often hit a Wall. Instead of feeling like your universe is conspiring to support you, it feels like every little win comes at an ever larger cost. Instead of achieving authentic success where you're also growing in consciousness, you create stress based success where the more you achieve, the less happy you become.

Before I take on a coaching client, they have to find and commit to at least two Big Wins: one external (such as increasing their income or growing their business), and one internal (such as reducing their stress or increasing their leadership). They have to back this up with a significant financial investment in our work together. And they have to be open to growth. When these three conditions are satisfied, I find that they consistently create radical breakthroughs – both externally and internally – because of a simple, profound truth.

The fastest path to any authentic, heartfelt goal involves growing in consciousness.

If a client of mine wants to make a million dollars in ways that are on purpose for them – terrific! The quickest way for them to do so usually involves facing their fears, resolving their inner conflicts, and growing their authentic leadership.

If a company wants to double their profits in ways that honor all their stakeholders – wonderful! The most efficient and sustainable way for them to do so usually involves growing their people, evolving their culture, and transforming their teams.

Sally was one of the youngest women to ever establish herself as a partner in a large consulting firm. She lived in a beautiful home and was making almost a million dollars a year. For work, she got to fly around the world having strategic meetings with top executives, all while traveling first class. Smart, beautiful, and successful, Sally had the world on a string.

Yet she was also working a minimum of 60 hours a week. She obsessively checked her emails and was completely wedded to her job. When we started talking, Sally's goal was to become a rainmaker in her firm – bringing in big clients, working less, and making more.

Yet as we started talking, the subject of relationships came up. Sally also wanted to be a wife and mother. She wanted to get married and have children. And given that she'd just turned forty, she was starting to worry that this might not happen for her.

After listening to her carefully, I offered this challenge: "Imagine that it's ten years from now, and you get to pick between two scenarios. In both, you've created a terrific marriage with a man you love. In the first case, your career has continued to skyrocket. We've helped you become a rainmaker and you're one of the top leaders in your firm. But you don't have any children. In the second, you've scaled back your career. You've taken on a smaller role with a significant pay cut. You and your husband have two beautiful children and you're still doing well financially, but you're not the high flyers you could have been. Two options. If you had to pick, which would you choose?"

The question brought her up short. It was more than ten minutes before she said anything. For ten minutes, Sally just thought. At first, she tried to deny the question, but she quickly caught herself. She saw how she'd been pushing it away for some time. Instead, Sally honored the question. She sat with it. She looked at the choices she'd been making and she looked at the fears she'd been hiding from.

As a result, Sally got clear that for her at this point, family was even more important than career. She saw how she'd gotten trapped in stress based success. And she recognized that her career goals were putting her greatest dreams at risk.

The reality was that if Sally wanted to honor her Big Win of having a family she needed to make it a top priority. Now.

As we checked in with her three voices, the voice of fear was primarily worried about loss and unworthiness. "What if I fully commit to my dream of having a family and fail?" "What will people think of me if I stop being such a superstar at work?" "How can I feel good about myself if

I'm no longer getting promoted?"

In contrast, Sally's voice of intuition didn't care about these things. It cared about the dream she'd had, ever since she was a little girl, of being a mother and having a family. Once we slowed down to really think about things, her voice of reason agreed.

As Sally owned this *Yes Yes Hell No!* she accessed her voice of reason to help her ground her decision and create a plan of action. She got clear that she needed to say no to some of her smaller dreams at work so she could say yes to her bigger dreams at home. Sally decided to create enough space in her life to build a relationship and a family. No more trying to squeeze it in between the cracks.

This led to some honest conversations with the managing partners at her firm. Sally scaled back her responsibilities, accepting that this would likely mean a pay cut for the upcoming years. Most important, she got clear on her priorities and redefined what success authentically meant for her.

As a result, Sally was able to build a great relationship with the man she'd been dating. She truly invested. And while it's too soon to know about her dreams of being a mother, they just got engaged and are happily planning their wedding.

This isn't to say that a Big Win can't involve money. A client named Julie was running an internet based training business when the great recession of 2007 hit. In the space of a month, her company's revenues dropped by half. Her first instinct was to drop our coaching as a way of propping up her cash flow. Yet as we slowed down and talked about it, she got clear that for her company to survive, she was going to have to transform her level of leadership. She came up with some goals that were heartfelt, specific, and scary.

And then we rolled up our sleeves and got to work.

Saving her company required deep surgery, both with *what* she'd been doing in her business and *how* she'd been doing it. Over the next 24 months, she restructured almost every aspect of the company. Before the recession, Julie had felt stuck between being greedy and selfish, or nice and self-sacrificing. Moving forward, she committed to building relationships based on Win/Win or No Deal. She let go of the customers, employees, and partners where this wasn't the case. She provided terrific service to those who stayed. She grew her leadership in profound ways. And after a few very scary quarters, she turned things around.

In doing so, Julie created one of the leading companies in her industry. It provides amazing value, generates abundant profits, and runs so smoothly that it requires less than twenty hours a week of her time. She actually got a bit bored with it. So she moved to Hawaii and now manages the company from there while pursuing her latest passion – the flying trapeze.

Authentic success comes from committing to goals that are aligned with your soul's path. Doing so lets you create money and meaning – success and fulfillment – all at the same time.

How do you do this? I don't get tired of saying it: keep looking for your *Yes Yes Hell No!* The voice of intuition will guide you to your highest priorities each and every time. And just as reliably, the voice of fear will let you know when you are growing outside of your comfort zone.

You certainly don't have to be poor to be happy. Remember, at the top of the ladder of consciousness, life shifts from being about either/or to being about both/and. At the top, you get to have your cake and eat it too. You get to create success on *your terms* and make it work *for you*, rather than getting stuck in an eternal rat race where you run, run, run until you die.

You can be a leader at work without having to sacrifice your family. You can be a parent at home without having to sacrifice yourself. The key is to pick goals that are heartfelt, specific, and scary, while limiting your commitments to what you can consciously handle.

When people first hear this statement they sometimes think it means that they need to quit their job and do something completely different. But there are two ways to create more heartfelt goals. You can either change the goal or change the way you're pursuing that goal. For example, if you're not inspired by your job, how could change the way you approach your job so that it creates more opportunities for growth, contribution, connection, and creativity?

As you commit yourself to heartfelt goals and authentic success, challenges come up. As you move through these challenges, you increase in consciousness and automatically expand your capacity for authentic leadership. You grow in your ability to craft creative Win/Win scenarios and relationships. You strengthen the quality of your presence. You master the art of creating real connections. And you get to harness the power of flow.

In turn, these gifts radically increase your effectiveness in the world. You'll get more done in less time. You'll provide higher value in anything you do. You'll create an even higher level of authentic success. And as you do so, you'll also open to the gift of creativity.

Chapter 21

The Gift of Creativity

"Learning and innovation go hand in hand. The arrogance of success is to think that what you did yesterday will be sufficient for tomorrow." ~ William Pollard

In this time of great change, innovation is no longer a luxury – it's a requirement. Gone are the days where we could just learn a trade, get a steady job, and do the same thing for a lifetime.

The middle class was built on the need for skilled, routine jobs in such realms as manufacturing, marketing, and management. It used to be enough just to show up each day and do what you were told.

No more. Average is over and the only real constant is change. This is true, not just at the top as with new strategies or acquisitions, but throughout an organization.

Innovation is the most important currency of the twenty-first century.

If you want to get ahead you need to be creative. You need to become a master of invention and an agent of change. You constantly need to be learning and creating new ways of adding value.

But here's the thing.

The faster things change, the more stressful life becomes. And after a point, stress makes you stupid.

Stress creates *activity*, but it destroys *creativity*. It causes smart people to do stupid things.

Remember, stress and scarcity register at the bottom of the ladder of consciousness. Wisdom, innovation, and creativity come from the top.

The paradox of innovation is that the more desperately you *need* to be creative, the harder it is to access. And the faster you need to learn and change, the more difficult these changes become.

In their book *Scarcity*, Sendhil Mullainathan, a Harvard economist, and Eldar Shafir, a psychologist at Princeton, describe this dynamic. Over the past years they've conducted experiments that move people into scarcity thinking and then they've measured the results. They found that the drop from neutral, average consciousness to a mentality of scarcity creates the equivalent of a loss of 13 to 14 IQ points.

Have you ever been seriously sleep deprived for a sustained period, let's say when dealing with a new baby? Do you remember how difficult it was to think clearly? The drop they measured, due to scarcity thinking, is even greater and more debilitating.

On the flip side, there are huge benefits in shifting from average consciousness to abundance consciousness. Genius resides at the top of the ladder, a place we all have the potential to access.

For me this phenomenon of diminished creativity under stress shows up most obviously in my writing. When my life gets too full and I start feeling stressed, the quality of my writing plummets. I'll either get writer's block where I can't write at all, or I'll get a bad case of "writing crap" where the words pile up on the page along with an increasingly unpleasant mental smell.

When this happens, I know that I need to slow down in order to speed up. I need to say no to more things that drain me and yes to more things that feed me, such as my family, meditation, and exercise.

Otherwise stated, I need to raise my level of consciousness. Then, something shifts. I move to a different place inside. My creativity emerges. I drop into my writing mode and the words begin to flow.

And as my wife will tell you, when this happens I become a *much* happier person.

Creativity comes from something greater than the mind. It comes through you, not from you. It's something you open to rather than something you make happen.

And while it doesn't show up on demand, creativity is far more likely to be forthcoming when you make the choices we've been discussing that take you to higher levels of consciousness. Remember, you cultivate this through an ongoing practice of taking Leaps of Faith based on finding your *Yes Yes Hell No!*'s.

The practice of leaping and being caught increases not only creativity, but also the capacity for other gifts such as intuition, innovation, and inspiration. The more you use your creativity, the more it flows through you. The more you listen to your intuition, the louder it speaks to you. The more you dare to innovate, the more inspiration comes to you with the next bright idea.

And then there's nothing to do but revel in the gift of joy.

Chapter 22

The Gift of Joy

"Pleasure is always derived from something outside you,
whereas joy arises from within." ~ Eckhart Tolle

Pleasure is a beautiful thing, but it's also fleeting. It's sourced from the senses and it's ruled by the law of diminishing returns. Eating one chocolate éclair is a delight. Eating a dozen is a disaster.

Pleasure makes for a great dessert, but a horrible meal.

Don't get me wrong. I love pleasure. I'm a huge fan. It's just that a life *ruled* by pleasure invariably leads to addiction and pain.

In contrast, there are no limits to joy. It's not fattening, immoral, or dangerous. It doesn't diminish or dissipate. Quite the contrary. In my experience, it just gets better with time.

These days, my wife and I seem to spend half our time wondering how our daughters can be so cute. No matter how much joy we experience with them, there always seems to be room for more.

Joy is one of the greatest gifts. It's one of the most delicious benefits of lifting in consciousness. It's one of the tastiest ways of knowing when you're on purpose, and it's one of the sweetest rewards for following your purpose and walking your path.

While pleasure comes from the body, joy comes from the heart and spirit. It's an inside job. It's a spring that never runs dry.

And it's absolutely delightful.

One of the most fascinating things I've experienced recently has been what I call my "happy limp noodle days." As far as I can tell, they happen when I experience a burst of growth and increased consciousness, and my body needs time to catch up and integrate these changes.

I'll facilitate a retreat, or lead a series of powerful coaching sessions, and then I'll have to go lie down and bliss out for a while.

I can't be sure of the exact purpose of these waves, but I have no doubt as to the quality of the experience.

Pure joy.

Nicole will walk in and I'll be on the bed meditating with my eyes closed and a huge, ecstatic grin on my face.

When this happens, it's not like I'm doing anything to create these feelings. I'm just floating in bliss. If anything, my voice of fear gets a bit freaked out by this sometimes. It tries to shut down the joy and get me back into action. But for better or worse, it's not able to do so. It's like I've taken a trip, and I just have to wait to come down.

No drugs required.

All because of my practice of finding and following my *Yes Yes Hell No!*'s.

"Pleasure's a Moth, that sleeps by day
And dances by false glare at night;
But Joy's a Butterfly, that loves
To spread its wings in Nature's light."

~ William Henry Davies

Section III

LEARNING TO RECOGNIZE THE MANY FACES OF FEAR

Chapter 23

The Many Faces of Fear

"I'm not afraid of death; I just don't want to be there when it happens." — Woody Allen

Yes, *Yes, Hell No!* is the key to making Big Decisions, to creating Big Wins, and to receiving more of everything you most want in life. It automatically comes with many gifts, including growth, connection, abundance, flow, gratitude, service, authentic leadership, authentic success, creativity, and joy.

Mastering this tool requires learning how to understand and accept your fears. It involves being able to hear that "Hell No!" inside and know what it really means. But here's the thing: our fears are sneaky.

The voice of fear tends to speak loud and clear when you're about to jump out of an airplane or speak in front of a large audience, but most of the time it's not so direct. It may put on a mask and masquerade as something else, or hide below the surface just out of sight.

I've mentioned that my wife and daughters love me so much that it scares me, and I do realize it's a quality problem. Still, it's a real challenge for me. Their love triggers my abandonment fears. A deep, primitive piece of me is scared that if things get too good, something really bad is going to happen. It's like my inner Charlie Brown won't let me really go for it because of a fear that the football's going to get yanked away and my heart will get broken again.

The thing is, my fears don't usually come in the front door and announce themselves by name. Oh, no. They're much too clever for that. Instead, they usually show up as patterns of overwork and overachievement. When things get too good and I'm thrown off-kilter, I seldom find myself saying "I'm scared that life is too good and my family loves me too much." Instead, my voice of fear says things like "I've got too much work to do! I'll never get it all done. I need to roll up my sleeves and get to it! In fact, I really should start working nights and weekends again, even if that means spending less time with my family."

The voice of fear comes up with reasons why it's not okay to relax, open my heart, and receive the love that's here for me. It tells a tale of worst-case scenarios.

The *story* my fears tell is that I need to work harder. The *reality* is that I'm scared of being hurt. And the *choice* I have, once I notice what's really going on, is whether I run away from my fears – or step toward them.

The voice of fear shows up in many ways – excuses, stress, procrastination, anger, insecurity, and self-judgment. Even when it does show up as fear, it usually doesn't tell the truth about what's scary. It often focuses on symptoms rather than the real roots of the issue.

It can be difficult, on your own, to distinguish fear from reason. This is one of those areas where a great coach or therapist can provide a lot of value. And it's also a place where a little knowledge can go a long way. So in this section let's take a look at the "Big Four" – the top four fears and the most common ways they show up.

Chapter 24

The Fear of Loss

"Dance as though no one is watching,
Love as though you have never been hurt,
Sing as though no one can hear you,
Live as though heaven is on earth." ~ Souza

Everybody dies. This simple truth causes no end of problems. The reality is that sooner or later, you will lose everyone that you care about in this world. And this is terrifying.

To experience life is to experience loss. Opening yourself to love means opening yourself to pain. And the more you care, the more vulnerable you are to being hurt.

I'd like to think that my abandonment fears are irrational. And in the short term, they are – there's very little risk that I'll lose my wife or daughters in the next few years. But over the long term, these fears are all too real.

This reality presents a few choices: Do you focus on the risk or the reward? Do you pay attention to the joy of today or the fears of tomorrow? Do you treasure what you have or obsess about what you don't?

Would you rather your life be long and miserable, or short and ecstatic? If you're like me, it depends on which voice is talking. The voice of fear worries about safety and wants to live as *long* as possible. The voice of intuition sings of joy and wants to live as *well* as possible. Then the voice of reason chimes in to argue for both.

Fear of loss shows up most clearly in relationships. Have you ever gotten upset with someone you love? You were probably following the voice of fear. The people we care about have the greatest ability to piss us off, precisely because of how much we care.

Remember, fear is a fight or flight reaction. When your fear of loss is triggered, you naturally go to one of two polarities. Either you pull away to protect yourself emotionally, or you attack to try and get the other person to change. You choose either *silence* or *violence*.

My tendency is silence. When I'm scared, I pull away. My whole family of origin does the same. We almost never express anger directly. We repress it instead.

Nicole's family does the opposite: they don't repress, they express. Instead of pulling away, they get their feelings out, even if that means going on the attack.

Silence and violence are two sides of the same coin. They're two ends of the pendulum as it swings from one

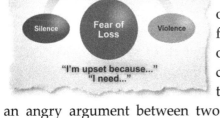

side of your emotions to the other.

Frustration is a sign of fear. When you're frustrated, you're scared of losing something you care about. This is why the fastest way to resolve an angry argument between two people is often to say "There must be something at risk here that we both care about. What is it?"

Even though they're sneaky, you'll find that your fears show up in predictable ways. Once you're on to them, you can see them for what they are, through *behaviors*, *feelings*, and *thoughts*.

Because the fear of loss shows up as behaviors of avoidance or aggression – as silence or violence – you can recognize it when either of these patterns shows up.

You can also learn to recognize its negative feelings. Insecurity, anger, frustration, guilt, unworthiness, and worry are all emotions rooted in fear.

Finally, you can notice the thought patterns that come with it. "I'm upset because…" Do you ever catch yourself thinking these words? The voice of fear often starts sentences this way. Another favorite is "I need…"

"I'm upset because you didn't come home when you said you would." "I need you to listen to me more." "I'm upset because my boss is an idiot." "I need a raise."

Where "I'd like" is a request, "I need…" is a demand. And "I'm upset because…" launches a statement of frustration and blame.

If you're demanding something or venting your frustrations, you probably fear that something is being threatened – something you care about deeply, such as a relationship, a job, or your self-esteem. So be kind to yourself when you catch yourself in this mode. Pause. Get curious. Listen to your voice of fear and look for its positive purpose. Like each and every other voice, it's trying to serve you the best way it knows how.

Chapter 25

The Fear of Unworthiness

"Sometimes the hardest part of the journey is believing you're worthy of the trip." ~ Glenn Beck

In high school, I was the kid that the chess team made fun of-literally. While other kids lettered in basketball or track, my varsity sport was chess – and I was the guy the other players made fun of. Needless to say, I was rather insecure. So as a teenager, I sat down one day, pulled out an empty, maroon, spiral bound notebook, and made a list of all the things I needed to achieve in order to have people like me. I figured out the things I needed to do in order to feel worthy.

And then I set to work.

Fourteen years and a ridiculous amount of energy later, I'd crossed everything off the list. I'd graduated with the top degree from the top university in my field. I'd competed athletically at the top levels. I'd bought a top car and moved into a top home. I'd spoken at the top conferences and raised money from the top venture capitalists. I'd cultivated some top friends and dated some top women.

That geek with a chess board grew up and he even learned to salsa dance.

Yet no matter how much I achieved, I couldn't seem to get rid of my fears. I flipped from insecurity (judging myself as less than others) to arrogance (judging myself as better), yet they were really the same thing. Just as anger is a cover for fear, arrogance is a cover for insecurity, and both come from the fear of unworthiness.

The fear of unworthiness often shows up as feeling insecure, worrying about rejection, or being oversensitive to what other people think. It's often accompanied with a strong need to please or a hunger for approval.

In terms of behaviors, this fear shows up as addiction to approval and achievement. The feminine side of this pattern is over-giving and approval seeking – doing most anything to meet the expectations of others. The masculine side is overachieving and status seeking – doing whatever it takes to be successful.

In terms of thought patterns, the fear of unworthiness shows up most commonly as statements that start either

with "I should...," "I shouldn't...," or "I'm insecure because..."

"I should make more money." "I shouldn't have so many fears." "I'm insecure because of my looks." "I should be nicer." "I shouldn't make mistakes." "I'm insecure because people don't seem to like me."

Your "shoulds" may sound rational, but they're not. They come from the voice of fear, not the voice of reason. They come from the almost universal fear of unworthiness.

Behind every "should" is a hidden "or else." There's a threat of punishment which we may or may not see. "I *should* make more money, *or else* I'm a bad provider." "I *should* be able to lose these extra ten pounds, *or else* I'm lazy and undesirable." "I *should* call my parents more often, *or else* I'm a bad daughter."

"I *should* do everything right, *or else* I'm not good enough."

These "shoulds" often become so ingrained that we accept them as truth. But they're not. They're just thoughts, and you don't have to believe every thought that you think.

Chapter 26

The Fear of Failure

"And the day came when the risk to remain tight in the bud
was more painful than the risk it took to blossom."
~ Anais Nin

What would you do if you knew you couldn't fail? That's one of my favorite questions. Think about it. What risks would you take if you weren't afraid of failing? What would you achieve? What would you create? What contributions might you make?

Your fear of failure keeps you small. It holds you back. It keeps you from owning your gifts and your greatness.

Yet, paradoxically, you may also rely on it to move you forward.

Does this ring true for you? Our fear of failure keeps us from playing big, but it also creates the stress we often rely on for our daily motivation.

What do you feel the most stressed about? Your job? Family? Health? Relationships? Money? Church? Your to-do list?

Stress has become such a fixture of our society that we rarely even question it. We assume it's something that happens to us, generated by outer circumstances. It's the normal result of all those people and problems we have to deal with each day.

"I'm stressed because I've got so much work to do." "I'm stressed because I don't have enough money to pay the bills." "I'm stressed because my boss might fire me." "I'm stressed because there aren't enough hours in the day."

"I'm stressed because..."
"I can't..."

Stress isn't something that just happens to us. It's another face of fear. When we have a stress response, we're usually afraid of failing in some way.

Stress is a socially acceptable name for fear. It's how we use negative fuel to create positive results.

Modern life is largely fueled by a combination of caffeine and fear. Have you noticed? Stress can be used to create amazing results. There's a reason why it's so ubiquitous. By and large, it's how we get things done.

The only problem is that stress hurts. It comes with steep costs. It's addictive. And over time, like all addictive substances, it becomes less and less effective.

Like many, perhaps the single biggest thing I learned in high school was how to use stress to create results. I didn't really enjoy my homework. And I didn't understand how learning the birth dates of dead people was going to help me date beautiful women or get a high paying job. But I desperately wanted to succeed, and I hated the idea of getting bad grades, so I learned how to work myself into a frenzy by focusing on my fear of failure.

Here's how it worked. In my mind, I'd figure out the minimum amount of time I needed to get a paper done. I'd use this to calculate the last possible time for getting started.

And then I'd wait.

As my deadline approached, I'd get more and more freaked out. I'd start thinking about how much my grades would suffer if I didn't finish my paper on time. I'd imagine bleak prospects for college and beyond. I'd bring out every fear of failure until l got really anxious. And eventually, I'd flip into "on" mode and buckle down to work, all stressed out and amped up.

Sometimes this worked and I'd get my papers done on time. They weren't brilliant, but they were finished. Other times, I'd miscalculate, or it would take me too long to get started, and my system failed me.

I remember one time in my junior year in a class where the teacher penalized us one letter grade for each day a paper was late, I didn't finish a paper on time. It was bad enough the first day I had to tell the teacher, in front of the whole class, that I had no paper to turn in. When I had to do so two days in a row, I was absolutely mortified. I felt like a complete failure.

I vowed never to let that happen again. I used the experience to get even more stressed about my homework. I beat myself up with it. It became the new fuel for my fears. Practice makes perfect, and I had lots of opportunities to practice being stressed before graduation.

I probably wasn't scared enough in high school, because I graduated in the bottom half of my class. Thankfully, I have a gift for succeeding when taking standardized tests and my SAT scores saved me. In college, I got better at being afraid and moved up to the top quarter. In grad school, I started to really master stress, and I began to truly feel successful. So much so that I started that high-tech software company as my first job out of college and raised millions. I was so stressed that I worked 90-hour weeks, and kept pushing myself harder and harder, until I burned out. Twice.

The first time, my adrenals stopped working. Since my body could no longer register stress, my motivation just stopped. Without my fear as fuel, we couldn't keep the company going. We fired everyone and sold our intellectual property (plus what was left of me and my adrenals) to a competitor. Our investors got about 30 cents on the dollar. With the new company, I managed to climb my way back to working 50 hours a week, and a decent level of stress, until our IPO when I managed to burn out for the second time.

What can I say? It's a gift.

My achievement addiction came out of my fear of unworthiness. I used my fear of failure to fuel my achievements until I became addicted to stress as well. I got to the point where I couldn't function without it.

The problem was that I also got to the point where I couldn't function with it, either. This is typical, because every time we use stress as a fuel source it extracts a cost.

According to the American Institute of Stress, between 75 to 90 percent of all visits to primary care physician's result from stress-related disorders. More than 100 million people per day are absent from work because of stress, at a cost of over $300 billion a year.

Our addiction to stress may be the primary reason why depression has doubled with every generation since the 1920s. It's certainly a big part of why Gallup consistently finds that 70 percent of full-time employees either hate their work or have disengaged from it to the point that they're costing their companies money.

Stress is painful. It causes us to feel scared and anxious. And over time, it becomes counterproductive, because the more we use it, the more we find ourselves procrastinating.

In high school, I procrastinated when it came to my homework. I always thought this was because I was lazy, unmotivated, or unworthy. It wasn't. Procrastination isn't a character flaw. It's the byproduct of an inner conflict: a part of us wants to do something and another part doesn't.

Procrastination is the automatic consequence of using fear as fuel.

Do you remember Pavlov's dogs? In this early psychology experiment, Ivan Pavlov would ring a bell each time he fed his dogs. He consistently paired the two events: Ring the bell, feed the dogs. Ring the bell, feed the dogs. Then one day, he rang the bell without feeding them and found that their mouths salivated anyway. The dogs had learned, in a deeply physical way, that "bell equals food."

The same thing happens whenever we get stressed about a task. Each time we use fear as fuel, we train our bodies to be afraid of that activity. We create resistance – at a deep, biological level – to the very thing we're trying to accomplish.

When this happens, we naturally feel conflicted. The voice of fear tells us that we have to do something or we'll fail. But this brings up our fear of that activity.

What's the easiest way to deal with this conflict?

Procrastinate. Put it off. Decide not to decide. Agree to worry about it tomorrow. Or the next day.

Or the day after that.

Starting in high school, each time I got stressed about my homework, I trained my body that "homework equals pain." I learned that homework hurts. Not because the homework was particularly painful, but because my fear of failure was.

This created a vicious cycle. Each time I used stress as a motivator, I created more resistance and an even stronger desire to procrastinate the next time I faced my homework. This forced me to create an even greater fear of failure, and to push things even closer to the deadline before I could amp up and "turn on."

The Vicious Cycle

I got to the point where I spent most of my life chasing my "on mode" – the state of being stressed enough to stop procrastinating and hit that glorious place of hyper-focus where it felt like I could do anything. But when I wasn't in that place, I had an even harder time being present and became ever less productive.

Even as I became more successful in terms of making money, I had a harder time functioning. I got to the point where I met the clinical criteria for ADD, and my father suggested that I explore medications. I put off paying my bills so much that I regularly had my utilities disconnected. I avoided going to the dentist, so I regularly had to have root canals. I lost all trust in my ability to create success without stress.

My life became one big oscillation between procrastination and overstress. I learned how to manage this pattern as well as I could. I figured out how to make it work for me, harnessing my fear of failure to create success.

But no matter how successful I became, I still felt bad. I still felt scared. And while I'd been raised to believe that I could do anything. I started shifting, after enough procrastination and failure, from "I can" to "I can't." I started giving in to my fears.

"I can't pay my bills on time." "I can't take care of my teeth properly." "I can't be present with other people." "I can't be trusted with responsibility." These self-judgments started to define my reality and identity. Not because they were necessarily true, but because of how powerful my fears of failure had become.

Chapter 27

The Fear of Success

"If at first you don't succeed, try, try again. Then quit.
There's no point in being a damn fool about it."
~ W. C. Fields

Failure is scary. That's obvious. What can be surprising is how deeply we're also scared of success.

There are many aspects to this fear. The first is social. When we're special, others may respect us. But they may also reject us.

My wife struggled with this challenge while growing up. While I'm admittedly biased, it remains true that Nicole is both unusually beautiful and talented. She's always picked things up quickly, and success has come naturally to her.

She also happens to be highly empathic. When Nicole walks into a room, she can literally sense what each person is feeling. She knows when other people are insecure, and she hates being the one who triggers their fears. So she's always held herself back.

With the exception of being a wife and mother, Nicole has never let herself truly excel. She's had a hard time owning her authentic greatness. She's always created just enough success so that people will like her. And people do. Within fifteen minutes of meeting her, people instantly want to be her BFF.

Beyond the social, our fear of success also has a psychological basis. It comes from the desire for safety that keeps us in our comfort zone. This isn't just a trick of the mind; it's related to our biological need for homeostasis.

The human body must regulate thousands of factors and keep each within a narrow range in order to stay alive. If the pH level in our blood gets too high – we die. If it gets too low – we die. If our body gets too hot – we die. If it gets too cold – we die.

This same pattern applies to our psychology. If our mood gets too low, we become depressed. If it gets too high, we become manic. We can become under-motivated and lazy, or over-motivated and exhausted. At both the biological and psychological levels, we're programmed to push back against any sudden changes and to return to the "set point" that we're used to. At an almost primal level, we're equally scared of having too little success and of having too much.

This may be why so many lottery winners lose their money or suffer other tragedies. In one famous study, researchers tracked the happiness levels of two groups of people who experienced a major life change. The first group won the lottery. The second group suffered a major accident that left them in a wheelchair.

Over the short term, the lottery winners experienced a marked spike in happiness while the paraplegics experienced a marked drop. But over time, both groups returned to almost exactly the same levels they'd had before the event. On the whole, the lottery winners reported being happier than the paraplegics – but only by a tiny amount.

Human beings have remarkable potential. Yet we rarely allow ourselves to stretch into fully becoming who we're meant to be.

As Marianne Williamson said, "Our greatest fear is not that we are inadequate, but that we are powerful beyond measure. It is our light, not our darkness, that frightens us."

"Yeah, but..."

I don't know why this is so. I just know that it is. The recesses of our minds are filled with shadows, and our most secret story is that we'll never be enough. The reality is that we are greater than we can imagine. But this journey of discovery evokes our deepest fears.

In terms of behavior, this fear of success shows up in two primary ways: as playing small and grandiosity.

Playing small is the most common. It shows up in many different ways, such as self-sabotage, resistance to change, playing it safe, and false humility.

Self-sabotage can be subtle, as when we forget about a tool we already have that would simplify a task. Or it can be glaringly obvious, as in the many times when I managed to shock Nicole into asking "what is *wrong* with you?!"

Resistance to change shows up as an attachment to comfort and a fear of growth. We refuse to take a good look at ourselves and go into patterns of denial instead. We defend and make excuses. The older we get, the stronger this resistance seems to be. Still, it can be worked through, one little leap at a time.

Another way of playing small is by playing it safe, where instead of stretching ourselves and going after inspiring intentions, we settle for small, safe, comfortable goals. Instead of pursuing our dreams, we tackle our to-do lists. Instead of trying to be the best we can be, we settle for mediocrity.

A fourth way of playing small is through false humility. Kristina is a new client, who has more degrees than almost anyone I know. She's a medical doctor, a licensed therapist, and a holistic healer. She has a remarkable ability to help diagnose the real roots of chronic illness, and to support people in creating permanent improvements in their health. She has the genuine potential to be a leader in her field. Yet when we talk about growing her practice and changing her fee structure, she tends to drop into this small, helpless energy of false humility. "Who am I to do that?"

The flip side of playing small is grandiosity, where we try to overcompensate for our fears instead of addressing them directly. Where arrogance is a cover for insecurity, grandiosity is a cover for playing small. It shows up when we react against our fears instead of learning how to release them. And it happens when we chase only the symptoms of success, rather than finding and pursuing what we truly most want in life.

This pattern of behavior shows up most commonly as either an achievement addiction or ungrounded goals. While I played small in relationships for many years, I became addicted to achievement in most of the other areas of my life.

For a while, this served me – it pushed me to grow in some remarkable ways. But it wasn't clean. I was overcompensating for my fears, both of failure and of success. So no matter how many symbols of success I collected, I still felt small inside. While I got a quick "hit" of self-esteem from each accomplishment, it faded quickly and left me craving more.

Walking away from my high-paying, high-powered career in Silicon Valley was the closest thing to heroin withdrawal I hope I ever have to experience. It didn't matter how much money I'd made or how much success I'd created – I still felt this overwhelming hunger for more, More, MORE.

I remember being on a 4-day SCUBA trip on the Great Barrier Reef, shortly after my decision to quit my job. I was learning to dive in one of the most beautiful settings on earth. Yet during our meal breaks on the boat, I kept trying to find ways to talk about work so I could find an excuse to bring up my accomplishments.

Grandiosity also shows up when we create ungrounded goals. I'm all for dreaming big, but when we fail to create a realistic path to success, unrealistic goals can be a way of talking big while playing small.

For example, I regularly talk with aspiring coaches who are currently making about $10,000 a year and plan to get to $100,000 - $150,000 a year in the next 12 months, without investing any money in building their business. They're courageously following their purpose and talking a great game while setting themselves up to fail.

In terms of language, the fear of success shows up most commonly as "Yeah, but…" "Yeah, I really want to have sex with you, but I'm not willing to be vulnerable or committed." "Yeah, I'd like to build a new company, but I don't want to risk failing." "Yeah, I know I've accomplished a lot, but I really need to do more." "Yeah, I see how badly I need change in my life, but I just don't have enough time or money."

"Yeah, I'd love to own my authentic greatness, but I'm scared of growth and change."

"Our greatest fear is not that we are inadequate,
but that we are powerful beyond measure.

It is our light, not our darkness, that frightens us.
We ask ourselves, 'Who am I to be brilliant,
gorgeous, handsome, talented and fabulous?'

Actually, who are you not to be?
You are a child of God.

Your playing small does not serve the world.
There is nothing enlightened about shrinking
so that other people won't feel insecure around you.

We were born to make manifest the glory of God within us.
It is not just in some; it is in everyone.

And, as we let our own light shine, we consciously give
other people permission to do the same.
As we are liberated from our fear,
our presence automatically liberates others."

~ Marianne Williamson

Section IV

TEN
STEPS
TO
MASTERY

Chapter 28

How to Make Great Decisions

"Life is the sum of all your choices." ~ Albert Camus

How do you make decisions? This may be the most important choice you'll make. How you answer determines how you live. The remaining chapters lay out a clear, proven technology for how to create Big Wins and make Big Decisions. These step by-step instructions will guide you in finding your *Yes Yes Hell No!*'s and then taking action on them, even in the face of your deepest fears.

One step at a time.

This tool works as a stand-alone process. It's also compatible with any values-driven approach you may already be using, such as the method taught in Stephen Covey's *7 Habits of Highly Effective People*, some tools from the school of Corporate Social Responsibility, or concepts from any number of religious traditions.

The core practice is simple. Find a Leap of Faith. Take it. Repeat.

> The following chapters break this practice into ten simple steps. The first three are foundational. They define your approach to life. They set up the essential preconditions for you to receive value from this tool.

1. Pick Your Paradigm
2. Create Your Compass
3. Upgrade Your Fuel Source

Then the next four steps teach you how to listen to the three voices, and determine whether a specific choice is a Tiger, a Wall or a Leap of Faith.

4. Make Friends with Your Fears
5. Take Action and Listen for Feedback
6. Ground Your Decisions
7. Question Deeply

Making Friends with Your Fears is the essential tool for releasing your fears, resolving your inner conflicts, and creating true freedom. It can be practiced on a regular basis each time you experience fear or conflict.

Then as you release your fears, the last three steps are the keys for turning your decision into committed, courageous action.

8. Commitment Creates Value
9. Receive Support
10. Pay It Forward

Each of these steps is explained in the chapters that follow, along with a set of simple workbook exercises you can use to put this tool into action.

To access the detailed, specific exercises that go with each of these ten steps, particularly if you chose the Red Pill, please download and print out the complimentary workbook at www. YesYesHellNo.com.

A young boy came to his Grandfather, filled with anger at another boy who had done him an injustice.

The old Grandfather said to his grandson, "Let me tell you a story. I too, at times, have felt a great hate for those that have taken so much, with no sorrow for what they do. But hate wears you down, and hate does not hurt your enemy. Hate is like taking poison and wishing your enemy would die. I have struggled with these feelings many times.

It is as if there are two wolves inside me; one wolf is good and does no harm. He lives in harmony with all around him and does not take offence when no offence was intended. He will only fight when it is right to do so, and in the right way. But the other wolf is full of anger. The littlest thing will set him into a fit of temper.

He fights everyone, all the time, for no reason. He cannot think because his anger and hate are so great. It is helpless anger, because his anger will change nothing. Sometimes it is hard to live with these two wolves inside me, because both of the wolves try to dominate my spirit."
The boy looked intently into his Grandfather's eyes and asked,
"Which wolf will win, Grandfather?"
The Grandfather smiled and said, "The one I feed."

~ "The Two Wolves," A Cherokee Story

Chapter 29

Pick Your Paradigm

*"The most important decision we make is whether we
believe we live in a friendly or hostile universe."*
~ Albert Einstein

Thanks to years of advanced training, Nicole and I have managed to conquer one of the biggest challenges of marriage.

I have learned how to put down the toilet seat – at least most of the time – and she's learned how to be okay with me when I don't.

Okay, it may sound silly, but it's actually a big deal, because it required us to get clear on what these things *mean*. When I forget to put the seat down, Nicole's fears sometimes tell her that it means I don't really care about her. And when she gets frustrated with me, my fears often say she doesn't care about me. But in the face of our fears, Nicole and I have chosen to believe that we're always being loved and supported. It may not always show up in the way we want or in the moment we want it – but it's always there.

In the face of our fears and frustrations, we've chosen to believe that we live in a friendly universe. We've committed to living from a positive paradigm.

Your paradigm is the basis for how you interpret the things that happen to you. At the core, it comes down to a decision about the world you live in: is it hostile or friendly?

Are people here to help, or are they out to get you? Do your challenges mean there's something wrong with you, or are they opportunities for learning and growth?

In the face of whatever happens to you, your paradigm determines how you interpret those events. Do you pick optimism or pessimism? Do you take ownership of your emotions, or do you play the victim? Do you practice acceptance, or do you rush to judgment?

When you get upset, which wolf do you feed?

While pessimism may seem the safer choice, it's not. As Dr. Martin Seligman explains in his best-seller, *Learned Optimism*:

> *"Why should we bother to learn to think optimistically? Isn't pessimism just a posture with no real effects? Unfortunately not. I have studied pessimism for the last twenty years, and in more than one thousand studies, involving more than half a million children and adults, pessimistic people do worse than optimistic people in three ways: First, they get depressed much more often. Second, they achieve less at school, on the job and on the playing field, much less than their talents would suggest. Third, their physical health is worse than that of optimists. So holding a pessimistic theory of the world may be the mark of sophistication, but it is a costly one."*

Your paradigm determines how you see the world and how you relate to others. It defines the range of choices you're able to consider. It determines the choices you're able to make.

When you're living from a place of fear and scarcity, it's hard to choose a paradigm other than Lose/Lose, Win/Lose, or Lose/Win. Win/Win doesn't make sense on the low end of the ladder of consciousness, and even little actions – like leaving a toilet seat up – can suddenly be a big deal.

This has a dramatic, negative impact on relationships and results. With a negative paradigm, couples get divorced because they don't really trust each other. Businesses fail because their employees don't genuinely care about their customers. And countries go to war because they interpret one another's actions in the worst possible light.

In contrast, when you're living from a place of gratitude and abundance, your paradigm naturally goes to either Win/Win, or Win/Win, or No Deal. High on the ladder of consciousness, Win/Win is the *only* thing that makes sense.

Your consciousness creates your choices.

When you're feeling scared, your primary options are fight or flight. When you're feeling secure and connected, you have a much broader set of choices.

However, your choices also create your consciousness. Even in the midst of anger, you have the power to choose your paradigm. Even when your fears take control, you have the choice as to which voice you feed.

Fear argues for a paradigm of pessimism. Intuition sings of optimism and hope.

Which do you choose? This is a master choice because it has ramifications for every choice you make from here on out.

So decide. What will you choose? Don't think in terms of a feeling or something that would be nice to experience. What will you commit to? Will you live in a world filled with abundance or one filled with scarcity? Is your universe conspiring for you or against you? These are pivotal questions. Answering them may involve a Leap of Faith.

Choose love or choose fear. While you may think that love is a feeling, it's not. Love *can* feel good, and it can be a gift we receive from others. But it's much more than that.

Ultimately, love is a choice, a commitment, and a level of consciousness. It's the ongoing practice of "choosing up" – each and every day.

It's one thing to understand this as an idea or a concept. It's another thing to truly get it in your body, and build your life around this choice. For me, my marriage with Nicole has been all about this practice. Yet I didn't fully learn this lesson until the third time that I almost derailed our courtship, and came inches from making the biggest mistake of my life.

This last lesson happened after fifteen months of dating, including three months of my committing to her to practice opening my heart and taking down the wall around my heart. Even after all the work I'd done, it had taken everything I had to start making friends with my fears of abandonment, and to even consider marriage as a real possibility. But I was still stuck on the question: was she the right woman for me?

During this time, I attended a two-day training with a coach named Steve Chandler. In the afternoon of the first day, we were joined by his coach, Steve Hardison, and each of us was given the opportunity to ask him one question. Most questions involved matters of business, coaching, or leadership. I planned to ask something along those same lines, but a very different question popped out of my mouth: "How can I know if Nicole is The One?"

Steve Hardison's response changed my life – but not because he gave an answer to that question. He helped me see that I was asking the wrong question. He helped me understand how I had been treating love as something that would happen to me based on picking the "right" person.

I heard Steve on a deep level. I got it: true love isn't a feeling.

Love is a choice. And it's a commitment. It's not something that happens to you, like falling in a pit. Instead, you create it, one day at a time, one decision at a time. It's a paradigm choice, about how we approach our lives.

Nicole is The One. How do I know? Because I chose her, and she chose me. I keep choosing her, and she keeps choosing me. Nicole is the love of my life because I'm committed to loving her. Loving Nicole is my paradigm. It's a master habit that I practice, each and every day, one choice at a time.

That's easy to say now. What I didn't know at the time was that while I was at this training, Nicole had gotten clear that she was done waiting for me. She wanted a man who would truly love and cherish her, and who was willing to fully commit his heart to her.

As much as she loved me, it was clear that I wasn't there.

After I got home from the training, I suggested that we go out for dinner to one of our favorite little cafés. Nicole seemed unusually distant, but I figured, hey – no big deal, I have plenty of time to connect with her. What I didn't know was that she was getting ready to start a big fight so we could truly end things. So after we had sat down and ordered our meals, she pushed "the button" – the one issue guaranteed to cause a fight between us.

"Yeah, but I'm not The One," she said, while bracing for the explosion.

In a completely logical, matter of fact way, I turned to her and shared my new discovery. "Oh, that was my mistake. I didn't understand what I was doing. I thought that finding The One was about finding the person who would make me happy in a safe and secure way. Instead, I realized it's a choice. I now know that you are The One, because I choose you to be."

"What is *wrong* with you!?" Nicole exclaimed.

"I was about to break up with you! And you just made this big change? When were you going to tell me?!?"

Thankfully, her frustration didn't last, we promptly made up, and shortly thereafter I proposed to her – twice, just to make sure it really sunk in.

In the end, there were two things that saved our relationship. First, I opened my heart enough to be able to truly feel my love for her. I found the *Yes Yes Hell No!* that had been hiding behind that inner titanium wall. And second, I took ownership of my decision. I realized that love isn't about safety and comfort and finding the right object. It's a choice. It's a commitment. It's a habit of consistently making great Big Decisions.

How do I know that Nicole is The One? Because I choose to love her. To the best of my ability. No matter how I'm feeling. Each and every day. Loving Nicole has become an essential part of my paradigm. It's not just what I do. It's who I am.

In the same way, I know that I live in a loving universe. How do I know? Because I choose to live there. It's my paradigm. It's the way I see the world. It's my home and it's my practice.

And I invite you to make it your practice as well.

"This man stood in front of a group of high-powered over-achievers and said, 'Okay, time for a quiz.' Then he pulled out a one-gallon, wide-mouthed Mason jar and set it on a table in front of him. Then he produced about a dozen fist-sized rocks and carefully placed them, one at a time, into the jar.

When the jar was filled to the top and no more rocks would fit inside, he asked, 'Is this jar full?' Everyone in the class said, 'Yes.' Then he said, 'Really?' He reached under the table and pulled out a bucket of gravel. Then he dumped some gravel in and shook the jar causing pieces of gravel to work themselves down into the spaces between the big rocks.

Then he smiled and asked the group once more, 'Is the jar full?' By this time the class was onto him. 'Probably not,' one of them answered. 'Good!' he replied. And he reached under the table and brought out a bucket of sand. He started dumping the sand in and it went into all the spaces left between the rocks and the gravel. Once more he asked the question, 'Is this jar full?'

'No!' the class shouted. Once again he said, 'Good!' Then he grabbed a pitcher of water and began to pour it in until the jar was filled to the brim. Then he looked up at the class and asked, 'What is the point of this illustration?' One eager beaver raised his hand and said, 'The point is, no matter how full your schedule is, if you try really hard, you can always fit some more things into it!

'No,' the speaker replied, 'that's not the point. The truth this illustration teaches us is: If you don't put the big rocks in first, you'll never get them in at all.'"

~ Stephen Covey

Chapter 30

Create Your Compass

"Good is the enemy of great. And that is one of the key reasons why we have so little that becomes great. We don't have great schools, principally because we have good schools. We don't have great government, principally because we have good government. Few people attain great lives, in large part because it is just so easy to settle for a good life." ~ Jim Collins

The next step to making a great decision is to get clear on what you most want, and why, so that you can put first things first in your life.

Most people know what they want. But few people know what they want *most*. The real test in life is not the choices we face between good and bad, it's our choices between good and better.

"Do you want the pleasure that comes from eating lots of ice cream or do you want a fit and healthy body?" "Do you want to squeeze in some more emails after dinner or do you want to spend more time with your family?" "Do you want to focus more on adding to your success or growing your consciousness?"

Without a strong awareness of and commitment to our highest values, we naturally become a slave to what's urgent instead of what's important. We sacrifice the great things in life for those that are merely good. We fail to put the big rocks in the jar first, and end up with just a pile of pebbles and sand.

In my coaching work, one of the most important things I do is to ask people three simple questions: "Where are you now?" "Where do you most want to be?" "What's in the way?" It constantly amazes me how much value people receive just from getting clear on their highest priorities.

So please. Slow down and give this step some thought. What is most important to you? What do you most want to create with your life? What are your strongest values and your highest priorities? These form your compass. Then this becomes a master tool you use to measure all your other goals and actions against.

There are two keys for Creating Your Compass. The first key is simple, yet often elusive.

Focus on what you *actually* want instead of what you think you *should* want.

So many people spend their lives trying to live up to a set of expectations that they inherited, instead of figuring out what's true for them.

These expectations can come from many sources – parents, friends, teachers, church, the media – and these can be great starting points. But if you want to make great decisions in life, you need to figure out what *you* really want. What do you value? What brings you happiness? What's your purpose? What makes your heart sing?

When I was at Berkeley, I was a teaching assistant for one of the hardest engineering classes on campus. Students had to pick a partner and then build different electronic devices – say, a universal TV remote control – from scratch, using only the most basic components. Some teams put in

30 to 40 hours a week, just on this class. Many teams never got their projects working at all.

It was like geek hazing, but with circuit boards instead of paddles.

In talking with the students, I'd often ask them what they were doing there. Why did they put themselves through such hell? Some students answered that they loved engineering, had a passion for electronics, and saw this class as an exciting challenge.

Others answered that their parents had pushed them into it. They didn't really like engineering, but their parents approved it as a well-paying career. So some students were suffering through each semester trying to meet their parents' expectations.

It will probably come as no surprise that the first group did much better than the second. Even more important, they were much happier. Having gotten clear on what they really wanted – not what they should want – they had this first key in hand, and that made all the difference. They enjoyed the challenge, while the other group dreaded it.

The second key for Creating Your Compass involves getting to the heart of what you care about most.

Focus on essence instead of form.

Like most people, you may habitually approach life from the outside-in. We're taught to think of all the things we need to *have*, in order to *do* the things we want to do, in order to *be* the way we want to be.

Values describe who we are. Goals describe what we want to have and do.

If you want to have a great life, create the practice of making your values more important than your goals.

For years, my version of this went as follows: "I need to have a great education, in order to get a great job, in order to make lots of money, in order to marry a beautiful woman, in order to feel loved and successful. And then I'll be happy!" My essential values were love and happiness. Yet I devoted most of my energy to my "in order to" goals, even when those goals took me away from the love and happiness I craved.

We're trained to set our sights on the ladder of success, believing this will somehow get us to the place of happiness and joy. This approach can sometimes work at a certain level, but it can also be hopelessly inefficient. It can easily lead to a wasted life; where we put so much energy into achieving the symbols of success that we miss out on the experiences of life we actually crave.

Instead of focusing on symbols and symptoms (form), figure out what it is you really want (essence) – and go for that. There are hundreds of ways to create the experiences you desire – including love, joy, connection, fulfillment, service, meaning, and purpose. You don't have to be the poster child for success before you can be happy and make a difference. Create the life you want today!

When you attach to a particular form ("I need to make this much money in order to find love," or "I need to weigh this many pounds in order to feel good about myself"), notice how easily you can get sidetracked. When you focus instead on the essence of what you want, you're much more likely to turn your intentions into reality. When one particular form eludes you, you can keep watching for other ways you can honor the essential quality you value. This way you can keep your eyes on the prize, no matter how many twists and turns you face along the path.

Then the next step is to Upgrade Your Fuel Source.

Chapter 31

Upgrade Your Fuel Source

"The first agreement is the most important one and also the most difficult one to honor. It is so important that with just this first agreement you will be able to transcend to the level of existence I call heaven on earth. The first agreement is to be impeccable with your word. It sounds very simple, but it is very, very powerful. Why your word? Your word is the power you have to create. Through the word you express your creative power. It is through the word that you manifest everything." ~ Don Miguel Ruiz

Your paradigm defines the world you live in. Your compass points towards where you want to go. Then the next step is to create the motivation you're going to use to move forward on your path.

In doing so, you can use either positive or negative fuel. As we explored in chapter 26, stress is how we use negative fuel to create positive results. And while a little stress can be productive, chronic stress makes us feel insecure, unworthy, unhappy, and possibly sick. It leaves us stuck in a trap where no matter how much we achieve, it never feels like enough.

Expectations are the primary cause of stress and insecurity. If you want to reduce your

**level of stress, reduce your expectations while
maintaining your goals.**

Expectations are
"shoulds." They're all
the things we think
should be different,
either in ourselves, in
others, or in the world. It
doesn't matter whether
our expectations are
good or bad. This isn't
about right or wrong. All expectations, no matter their
content, create stress. They create a gap, between how we
think the world *is* and how we think it *should be*. This gap is
automatically filled with stress, insecurity and unhappiness.
It's the way our brains work. It's the mechanism through
which we turn fear into fuel. It's easy to use. But it comes
with a steep price.

Mark was deeply insecure and harshly self-critical. No
matter what anyone else said, he always felt he was a failure.
During a coaching session, we slowed down and asked his
voice of fear some questions. "What is the purpose behind
all these self-judgments and failed expectations? How are
you serving Mark the best way you know how?"

His voice of fear responded, "Without me, you wouldn't
get anything done. My judgments and expectations are the
only reason you have any motivation at all." Mark hadn't
learned how to generate enough positive motivation, so
stress and insecurity was what he had left.

**Stress is what we fall back on when we don't trust
that we can get our needs met in positive ways.**

In contrast, positive motivation starts with heartfelt goals. It's hard to get excited about something you don't really want. Genuine motivation comes from genuine desire. Then there is one essential key for turning this wellspring of energy into a source of fuel you can trust.

Be impeccable with your word.

Consistent, positive motivation comes from building a habit of making and keeping wise agreements. Instead of setting yourself up to fail via unrealistic expectations and over-commitment, be honest about what you can really take on. Create clean and clear agreements that move you towards an authentic goal, and follow through on them. Doing so will change your life in remarkable ways.

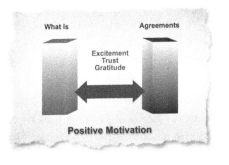

Where negative fuel creates stress, insecurity, and unhappiness, positive fuel creates excitement, trust, and gratitude.

Upgrading your fuel source is an incremental process. It's about letting go of negative habits and replacing them with more positive ones.

Expectations are like the junk food of motivation. Making and keeping wise agreements is like eating well and going to the gym. It can take some effort at first, but over time these new habits take on a life of their own. The key is to take things one step at a time. If each month you reduced your negative motivation by 3 percent and increased your positive motivation by the same amount, within a year you would have transformed your life.

YES YES HELL NO!

Here's an extremely powerful exercise for doing so. Again, this isn't a quick fix. It's something to practice until it becomes a natural part of your regular habits.

The exercise is based on asking two questions. "What's enough?" and "What's exciting?"

With the first question, the goal is to reduce your expectations. How can you make it as easy as possible to succeed each day? For example, how much income do you need to earn in order to cover your family's basic needs? That's enough. How much attention do you need to give your children in order to let them know they are loved? That's enough. How much do you need to provide your clients in order to give them value? That's enough.

This isn't about settling. It's not about laziness. And it's not about giving up. It's about upgrading your fuel source, so you can create even more of what you most want in life, and be of even greater service in the world.

Letting go of our expectations can be scary. It's a Leap of Faith.

For me, it triggers some of my deepest fears. "If I stop pushing so hard, I'll turn into a lazy slob." "If I don't make more money, my wife will stop loving me and leave me for someone else." "If I take a long vacation, I'll never want to go back to work."

If you really sit with this first question and do the work of facing your fears and letting go of your expectations, you'll naturally start to experience a sense of spaciousness. Your consciousness will shift from scarcity to abundance. Then, from this new place, you have the opportunity to genuinely explore the second question. "What's exciting?"

168

It's much easier to take risks when you feel like a success than when you feel like a failure. It's much easier to come up with inspiring goals when you trust that you already are enough.

So take yourself off the hook. Let go of your expectations. Decide on some honest, minimum standards – what truly is enough? Take care of those needs. Then from that place, dare to dream.

And dream big.

Chapter 32

Make Friends with
Your Fears

"What is needed, rather than running away or controlling or suppressing or any other resistance, is understanding fear; that means, watch it, learn about it, come directly into contact with it. We are to learn about fear, not how to escape from it." ~ Krishnamurti

Pick Your Paradigm. Create Your Compass. Upgrade Your Fuel Source. These first three steps provide the foundation for any heart-centered journey. They establish a way of being in the world. Then from this solid place, let's walk through the specific steps for discerning which voice is which, and for using this information to make Big Decisions and create Big Wins.

In connecting with the three voices, start with the voice of fear. This allows you to honor and appreciate it, and also to isolate it, because it tends to drown out the other voices. When you listen to it, accept it, and have it speak as fear rather than letting it pretend to be something else, it tends to quiet down.

In meeting fear, you want to come from a place of understanding and acceptance. Fear's job is not to stop you – it's to warn you. Like all of your voices and all the different aspects of you, it has a positive purpose behind everything it does.

The problem is that, sometimes, with the most positive of intentions, your less conscious aspects create less than positive results.

So let's get curious. What does your voice of fear have to say? While this may sound a bit strange at first, the goal of this step is to create a literal dialogue between you and your voice of fear.

The first step is to create a *connection* with this voice. The process starts by finding where your fears are showing up in your body. Think about the Big Win you're thinking of creating, or the Big Decision you're planning on making. Notice any negative or stressful emotions that arise and notice where they are located in your body.

Place one hand on that area of your body. Then check in again. Is this the only place in your body where you're experiencing fear? If there is a second place in your body where fear or tension is showing up, place your other hand there. Then pause, take a breath, and ask this voice a question.

"What are you feeling or what do you want to share with me?"

Listen for the answer. If you're not able to do so at first, keep practicing, or find someone who is trained in this technique that can help you. With the right support, almost anyone can learn how to make this connection.

Once you've created a connection with the voice of fear, the second step is to create an *understanding* of this voice. Ask yourself some or all of the following questions and listen to the answers. Keep going until you feel that you've fully heard what the voice of fear is trying to share with you.

"What are you trying to warn me about?"
"How are you trying to protect me?"
"What are you afraid it would it mean if that happened?"
"What is the worst case scenario that you're worried about?"

The third step is to create *acceptance* of this voice. Ask the following questions and listen to the answers. Behind each warning is a positive value or goal, such as safety or freedom. What are they? Get curious.

"How are you serving me the best way you know how?"
"What is your positive purpose?"
"In addition to safety, what other goals or outcomes are you trying to help me create?"

In asking these questions, the most important thing is the energy with which you ask them. As you ask them, are you feeling judgmental or defensive, where you're trying to attack your fears and get rid of them? Or are you able to meet your voice of fear with love and acceptance, such as you might give to a five year old who feels scared and alone? Even if the fears don't sound rational, can you understand how a frightened child might feel this way?

Then the fourth step is to *make an offer of friendship*. This starts by finding one or more positive values which both you and your voice of fear can agree on, such as safety, success, freedom, or connection. Then once you have a set of shared goals, you can offer a clean, open invitation of friendship, where you ask the voice of fear is it would be willing to work together with you to create these goals in ways that may be scary, but are also safe.

If you offer this as a genuine question, where you're okay with hearing either a yes or a no, the voice of fear will often accept your offer. Then you can complete this process by asking it what it would need from you in order to do so.

> *"I appreciate how you've been working so hard to create these goals, in the best way you know how. Would you be willing to work together with me, as friends, to move forward with our goals in ways that might be scary at times yet are also safe?"*

> *"What would you need from me in order to better do so?"*

> *"Is there anything else you want to share with me?"*

This process might seem a bit strange at first, but with a bit of practice, most people find that it becomes a simple, straightforward, and remarkably profound exercise.

Here's a sample dialog between me and my voice of fear, regarding the blocks and conflicts that show up in relationship with my wife.

This process started with me noticing that I was feeling a defensive, insecure need to pull away from my family and into my work. Rather than just giving into the fear, I paused and noticed that my stomach felt upset and the area around my heart felt tight and constricted. I put one hand on each of those areas and engaged in the following conversation, from a place of acceptance and understanding.

> *Me: What are you feeling or what do you want to share with me?*

> *Fear: I'm scared. It's not safe to be so open. Something bad is going to happen, and you're going to get hurt.*

Me: What are you trying to warn me about?

Fear: Danger! Danger! It's not safe to be so open and vulnerable!

Me: Okay. I hear you. How are you trying to protect me?

Fear: I'm trying to keep you safe from being hurt and abandoned. I'm worried that Nicole is going to stop loving you and leave you behind.

Me: What are you afraid it would it mean if that happened?

Fear: I'm afraid it would mean that you're unworthy of love and you're going to die alone.

Me: How are you serving me the best way you know how?

Fear: I'm trying to keep you safe.

Me: What is your positive purpose? In addition to safety, what other goals or outcomes are you trying to help me create?

Fear: I'm trying to create more love and connection.

Me: Okay. I totally get that. I would also like to create love, connection, and safety, all at the same time. I appreciate how you've been working so hard to create these goals in the best way you know how. Would you be willing to work together with me, as friends, to move forward with these goals in ways that might be scary at times yet are also safe?

Fear: Yes, I'd be willing to do that. I know we keep having this conversation and I appreciate that. I'm sorry that I sometimes get so scared and out of control.

Me: I appreciate you and I'm grateful for the relationship we're building. What would you need from me in order to better do so?

Fear: Can you check in with me more regularly? Say once a week?

Me: I can do that. How about if I put it in my calendar for a short, weekly check in on Sunday nights?

Fear: That feels good.

Me: Is there anything else you want to share with me?

Fear: No. I'm good now. Thank you for listening to me.

This process starts with awareness. When you experience fear or other negative emotions, pay attention. Notice. Where do you feel it in your body? And how do you tend to react? Do you tend to fight, flee, or feed those fears?

Then the next step is acceptance, which is an incredibly powerful response to fear, but which is exactly the opposite of how most of us respond.

When you fight your fears, you attack them and try to overcome them – you invalidate them or push your way through them.

When you flee from your fears, you avoid them in the hope they'll go away. You may go into denial or do something to distract yourself. You may numb out, perhaps by consuming something that momentarily makes you feel better.

When you feed your fears, you give them energy, focus on them, and indulge in them. Anytime you use stress as a fuel source you're doing just that.

All three of these choices involve meeting fear with fear, and over time this can only make our anxieties worse.

In contrast, acceptance is an act of love. It's a gift of caring. It's a radically different response. At times it can feel weak or even foreign. But it's one of the most powerful and courageous decisions you can make in response to what scares you.

When you shift from trying to conquer your fears, to genuinely making friends with them, everything changes. Your fears give up much of their energy, and sometimes the fear goes away entirely. This makes it much easier to listen for the voice of Intuition, as well as to take committed action.

A number of years ago, I worked with a client who provided a dramatic example of this shift. In college, John was a football star, and he almost made it to the pros. Today, he's a single father with a handsome son. He's charismatic, good looking, brilliant, and strong. He has an unusual ability to connect with people. And he's a successful entrepreneur.

When I worked with John, he was one of three partners in a consulting firm. As part of our work together, we had scheduled a one-day strategic planning session for the four of us to attend.

A week before that meeting, John experienced a wave of major depression. All of a sudden, he could barely get out of bed. His partners supported him by getting him to see a psychiatrist and a therapist, and they helped take care of his son. Bolstered by this support, Mark started coming out of this wave of depression and we decided to go ahead with our meeting.

The day arrived and all three partners showed up at my home. However, within 15 minutes, John was curled up on the couch in my living room, crying. 250 pounds of muscle. In a ball. Sobbing.

We spent the next two hours focused on one thing – helping John connect with his fears and self-judgments, and listening to them with acceptance. At first, he had tremendous resistance. His whole life had been built around fighting through obstacles. To him, fears were enemies and tears were a sign of weakness. He had been trained that every challenge was something to be conquered.

Yet with time and patience, he was able to practice acceptance – and as he did the wave of sadness lifted. We got back to our strategic planning work and started moving ahead.

Then around 4 o'clock in the afternoon, John went into my kitchen to throw something away. As he was walking back into the living room, another wave of depression hit him. Mid-stride, he crumpled to the floor, pulled himself into a fetal position, and started crying again. I stayed where I was. Without making it a big deal, I asked some questions that helped him accept the sadness and fear, rather than fighting it or making it wrong.

He mustered up the courage to let himself go fully into this flood of feelings, with acceptance instead of judgment, and within five minutes it was gone. He got back up and we finished our work. Where the first wave of depression had knocked him out for a week, the second took two hours, and the third washed through him in minutes.

That's the power of Making Friends With Your Fears.

In a recent training, a woman named Anne volunteered to model this process in front of the audience. As part of the seminar, she had identified a heartfelt, specific goal that scared her – a Big Win that was also a *Yes Yes Hell No!* As she thought about committing to her goal, an intense level of fear came up for her, which she described as a "9" on a scale of 1 to 10. We spent about eight minutes walking her through this process, and by the end her fear had dropped to a "3" on the same scale.

Of all the tools in this book, this is one of the most powerful. I'm regularly surprised at how deep and consistent the results are that people receive from using it. At the same time, this is also the tool that most often requires live coaching or training to truly master. It's a skill, and mastering it does take some practice. So please, try it out, and if for some reason you're not able to get it to work for you right away, please feel free to visit *www.YesYesHellNo.com* to receive additional support in learning how to master this tool and make it your own.

Chapter 33

Take Action and Listen for Feedback

"The intuitive mind is a sacred gift and the rational mind is a faithful servant. We have created a society that honors the servant and has forgotten the gift." – Albert Einstein

Intuition isn't doled out to a few special people. We all have it. It's just that few of us have been taught how to recognize and use it. If you don't know what intuition is or how it works, it can be harder to access. However, even if you don't understand intuition, you're probably already using it, at least some of the time, without realizing it.

While it can show up in different ways for different people, intuition primarily functions like the hot and cold game that children play. Do you remember that game? A group of kids will pick something that's "hot," such as a lamp or a chair. Then another child will walk around the room. When she walks in the direction of the hot object, the group claps their hands and yells, "Warmer!" and increasing variations – "Hotter, burning hot, on fire!" When she walks away from the object, the group stops clapping and says, "Colder!" and decreasing variations – "Ice cold, freezing!" This continues until she touches the right object and everyone cheers.

The best way to listen for intuition is to Take Action and Listen for Feedback. The first step is to do something. This can include declaring an intention, taking a step in a given direction, or "leaning in" to an opportunity.

The second step is to pay attention to your body. What do you feel in response to your action? Do you feel contraction? Does your gut clench up or your throat constrict? If so, that's probably fear speaking. Does your heart open up? If so, that's probably intuition saying "Warmer!"

As you've been reading this book, you've probably had moments when something just resonated with you – as if somehow, somewhere in your body, the words just felt like wisdom to you. So pay attention. Where did you feel that sensation? What did it feel like? Go back and read a few of those passages again and notice how and where that feeling of resonance shows up for you. That's your voice of intuition guiding you in response to encountering a concept that has value for you.

Elizabeth is a best-selling author and the founder of one of the world's largest coach training institutes. Over the years she has helped certify thousands of professional life and executive coaches. When she asked me to coach her a few years ago, I was a bit shocked and scared. My voice of fear had a whole list of reasons why I wasn't ready to work with her. "She's so much more senior than me!" "Who am I to coach her?" "What if I screw up?"

Rather than take my fears at face value, I recognized them for what they were. I made friends with them, listened to them, and then took the next step – I moved into action. I didn't simply meditate and wait for an answer.

The question to be answered was, "Do we want to work together or not?" I decided to try it out. We scheduled a few coaching sessions in which we were able to connect and have the experience of working together, so that both of us could collect information on whether or not the choice made sense.

As we proceeded, my voice of intuition lit up. In my body I felt a sense of joy and positivity centered in my heart. Each time we talked, the conversation felt connected, and we regularly moved into an experience of flow.

We also created enough experiential "data points" about our ability to work together for me to be able to ground the decision rationally. I got to the place where I believed we could team up to create value for her.

As we leaned in to this opportunity, I got a very clear *Yes Yes Hell No!* And so did she. So we went for it. We coached together for 18 months with some very powerful results.

Ironically, one of the biggest things we did was help her learn how to better recognize and trust her voice of intuition. While she had already developed a strong connection to her inner truth and frequently used it to help her make decisions, she didn't think of herself as being particularly intuitive.

"I don't really have intuition," Elizabeth would say in one breath, and then in the next she'd share something like, "There was something in me that just knew I needed to work with you." She'd talk about what "resonated" with her or what she was feeling "called" to do. She'd explain that a decision just didn't "feel right." Ah, but what she really wished for was a clear connection to her voice of intuition.

Like many, Elizabeth didn't understand how intuition works. She was looking for a voice that would tell her what she should do, like Moses being sent up the mountain. But at least in my experience and observations, that's not how this "still, small voice" functions.

For me, intuition shows up as a feeling of joy and connection. It's a sensation of light that I experience in my chest and head. After years of practice, I still have a hard time finding the exact language to describe it, but there's no question when it's present.

When I'm listening to clients, some things they say will make them feel like they light up more than others. And when I take action on something that's on course for me, my heart feels more open and I feel more connected and peaceful.

The voice of intuition responds to action. It shows up primarily as sensations in the body rather than as thoughts in the mind. It lights up around choices that are on purpose, and if taken, would have the potential to move us up the ladder of consciousness.

Intuition doesn't tell us what destination we *should* choose. It tells us about a direction we *could* choose that's in alignment with our highest good.

The voice of intuition doesn't get scared or judgmental. It doesn't get angry or upset. It doesn't yell or scream. If you're feeling any type of negative emotion, you can bet that's the voice of fear. With intuition, off-course decisions might show up as a thud or sense of disconnection, but rarely as a sense of alarm.

Furthermore, intuition tends to be less concerned with notions of truth or right versus wrong. It lights up around wisdom and ideas that have value. Where the voice of reason deals with beliefs, facts, and information, the voice of intuition deals with love, growth, and transformation.

If the whole realm of intuition feels foreign or seems beyond your grasp, don't worry. There's a whole set of exercises and tools you can use to develop the skill of feeling into your fears and to get clear on how your intuition shows up for you.

Chapter 34

Ground Your Decisions

"The elevator to success is out of order. You'll have to use the stairs... one step at a time." ~ Joe Girard

Once you've found something that's both scary and exciting, that both triggers your fears and makes your heart sing, then it's time to ground your decision.

Reason's first job is to check for real and present dangers. This ensures that your Leap of Faith isn't happening from an actual physical cliff. It watches out for the stripes, claws, and fangs of a real Tiger.

Reason's second job is to prioritize your energies, so they're in line with your top values and goals. As you practice this tool, you'll find yourself encountering ever more potential Leaps of Faith. These are opportunities, not obligations. So which ones matter most? This is where your compass comes in. Check each

Take Small Steady Steps Towards
Big Inspiring Intentions

The Key to Success

Yes Yes Hell No! against it. How do they match up?

Locating and choosing a Leap of Faith is half the job. You now know *what* you want to do. Then reason's third task is to help you Ground Your Decision by clarifying *how* to move forward in the easiest and most efficient ways possible.

To achieve this, combine large intentions with small steps. This is one of the most important keys to success. However, it's the opposite of what most people do.

Do you ever set big, overwhelming goals or else limit yourself to small, uninspiring intentions? Tiny intentions are things you're sure you can achieve, but giant goals that you try to accomplish all at once are a set-up for failure. "Before summer, I'm going to lose 30 pounds. I'm going on a strict diet and joining a gym. I'm committed!"

This is a big, inspiring goal, and well-conceived in many ways. For most people, it would qualify as heartfelt, specific, and scary – a great example of a *Yes Yes Hell No!* – and it's paired with a plan of action.

But there's just one problem with this plan. It's pretty much guaranteed to fail.

Not because these are the wrong steps, but because they're the wrong size. "Go on a diet, join a gym, and keep up the new regime until I've lost 30 pounds." It's like trying to scale a tall building in a single bound. It might work for Superman, but not for the rest of us.

When instead you proceed step by step, every step is an opportunity to succeed and to feel good about your progress. It's a chance to build momentum. If there are only a few huge steps, then there will be many more opportunities to fail than to succeed. Each time you gaze at a plate of chocolate cake or push the snooze button when it's time to get up for the gym, you have another brush with failure.

And how often do you get to succeed? Exactly once – when you reach your goal.

Ouch!

Once you've checked for Tigers, Grounding Your Decision involves creating a plan of action based on small, steady steps.

When you start, you don't need to know what each and every step will be. To a certain extent, the path reveals itself as you walk it. Progress includes learning and course-correction.

However, you do want to choose the steps you're going to start with which will move you toward your goal, in solid, steady, measurable ways.

For example, here's a more grounded plan for losing weight. "I'm going to lose at least 3 pounds a month for the next ten months. To do this, I'm going to limit myself to, at most, one treat a day, and I'm going to work out at the gym at least three times a week."

With this plan, there are many more opportunities for success. Did you go to the gym at least three times this week? Success! Did you limit yourself to at most one treat today? Success! Did you lose 3 pounds in the last month? Success!

You can achieve remarkable things when you take small, steady steps toward big, inspiring intentions.

I stumbled upon this lesson when I was ten years old, and it cost my neighbors almost two hundred dollars. I was in fifth grade and I saw a flyer at school for the American Diabetes Association's annual bike-a-thon. First prize was a brand new bike worth $300. Second prize was a portable TV worth $200. And third prize was a portable stereo worth $100.

These prizes were golden for a ten year old kid from the cornfields of Illinois. And hey! Who could say no to such a good cause? Talk about a Win/Win!

So I started going door to door to prey on my neighbors. Many of them pledged to donate 10 to 30 cents for each mile that I rode, probably thinking "How cute. What a sweet kid. I can certainly afford a couple of dollars!"

When the day of the race came, I got on my little blue battered ten-speed bike and checked in at the nearby park. The volunteers explained that they'd set up a six-mile course with checkpoints every two miles. I could just ride my bike in a loop for as many miles as I wanted to go.

So I set out. And every two miles, I succeeded. I'd ride into a checkpoint and people would cheer for me. Yay! How exciting! Then someone would make a mark on my pledge sheet, and I'd set off for the next stop – where people would cheer for me again!

This was so much fun that I just kept on riding until someone told me it was time to stop.

At which point I'd ridden 50 miles.

I rushed home, proud as a peacock, to tell my mom. I'll never forget her reaction. "Are you okay?!? Did you hurt yourself? Let's get you upstairs so you can lie down!" Like my poor, unsuspecting neighbors, she was shocked at what I'd done.

But they all paid up, and I won a brand new stereo for my room.

So how do you actually put this into practice? How do you turn an inspiring intention into a string of small, steady steps? The key is to break your big goal into a series of smaller goals ("I'm going to lose at least three pounds a month for the next ten months"), and then to create a plan of action that includes *systems*, *practices*, and *skills*.

A *system* is a formula for how to do something. It's a recipe for a cake, a plan for a business, or the instructions for that frustrating toy you bought with "some assembly required." A great example is the operating manual for a

McDonald's franchise. Each step of each process – from making fries to cleaning bathrooms – is laid out in detail. These systems are what allow minimum-wage employees to create consistent, repeatable results, anywhere in the world.

"To lose weight, I'll eat less and exercise more." That's a proven system for success.

If you want to do something new, start by finding role models – people who have done something similar – and learn their systems. *Adopt* what they've done, and then *adapt* their formulas and make them your own.

Then once you have a system you trust, it's time to create new *practices*. Turn your goal into a series of regular habits that you focus on each week. "I hit the gym and exercise at least three times a week, and I eat, at most, one treat a day." Then keep building these habits, one success at a time, until they become automatic and take on a life of their own.

If you want to change your life, change your habits. One day at a time.

Then the third step is to develop the necessary *skills*. If you want to learn tennis, you must be able to hit the ball. If you want to play the piano, you must be able to learn the notes. If you want to be a web programmer, you must be able to code HTML.

"To help me lose weight, I'm going to learn how to cook meals that are both healthy and tasty." That's a skill.

Every area of life – be it work, art, self-care, relationships – has a set of systems, practices, and skills that form the foundation for success. What's your heartfelt, specific, scary goal? Can you find someone who has mastered that area of competency? Then how can you connect with them and learn the systems, practices and skills that they've found essential to their achievement?

Chapter 35

Question Deeply

"A thought is harmless unless we believe it. It's not our thoughts, but our attachment to our thoughts, that causes suffering. Attaching to a thought means believing that it's true, without inquiring. A belief is a thought that we've been attaching to, often for years." ~ Byron Katie

"Yeah, but I don't have what it takes." "Yeah, but I don't have the time or the money." "Yeah, but it's not what my parents think I should do." "Yeah, but it's not right for me to be so selfish." "Yeah, but I'm not allowed to do that." "Yeah, but who am I to do something so amazing?"

Remember: Fear is sneaky. The more important something is to you, the deeper and more challenging your fears can be, and the more often they try to masquerade as truth.

So once you've found your Leap of Faith and Grounded Your Decision, it's time to look at all those "yeah, buts" – all the excuses that *sound* so reasonable, but keep you from creating your dreams, claiming your authentic greatness, and living your purpose.

When the voices of fear and reason get mixed up together, the result is a *judgment*. A judgment is a thought or belief sourced from a place of scarcity and fear.

When you give your judgments energy – by repeating them or believing that they're true – you experience negative emotions, such as fear, insecurity, upset, guilt, anger, sadness, and shame. Fear creates judgments and judgments create fear.

Some of the most common judgments include expectations ("I should…," "I need…," or "I have to…"), excuses ("Yeah, but…" or "I can't…"), and blame ("I'm upset because…").

Here are a few of my deeper judgments. "If I'm going to succeed, I need to work all the time." "To get enough clients, I have to be the best at what I do." "I should be working harder." "Yeah, but if I keep this up, I'll burn out again." "I'm upset because I never have time to hang out and have fun." "I can't risk burning out again, because then I won't be able to support my family and I'll lose their love and respect."

It hurts to be inside my head sometimes, especially when I've got one foot on the gas and the other on the brake. I routinely think I need to be working harder while also worrying I'll push too hard and burn out again.

Thankfully, I've learned how to Question Deeply, and that makes all the difference.

The purpose of this practice is for you to separate the *content* of your thoughts from the emotional *energy* of your fears. It's to get clear on the difference between the three voices, rather than take everything that happens inside your head at face value. Like a popular bumper sticker I saw once read:

You don't have to believe everything you think.

There are three essential steps to this process of Questioning Deeply: *ownership, acceptance,* and *inquiry.*

QUESTION DEEPLY

Ownership is the practice of taking 100 percent personal responsibility for all your emotional reactions. It's the shift from being a Victim of the world – "I'm upset because of all the bad things that have happened to me," to being an Owner of your life, recognizing that your feelings aren't created by what happens to you, but by your judgments *about* what happens to you.

This profound truth is illustrated by the Taoist parable of a man and his lost horse.

A man named Sei Weng owned a beautiful mare which was praised far and wide. One day this beautiful horse disappeared. The people of his village offered sympathy to Sei Weng for his great misfortune. Sei Weng said simply, "That's the way it is."

A few days later the lost mare returned, followed by a beautiful wild stallion. The village congratulated Sei Weng for his good fortune. He said, "That's the way it is."

Sometime later, Sei Weng's only son, while riding the stallion, fell off and broke his leg. The village people once again expressed their sympathy at Sei Weng's misfortune. Sei Weng again said, "That's the way it is."

Soon thereafter, war broke out and all the young men of the village except Sei Weng's lame son were drafted and killed in battle. The village people were amazed at Sei Weng's good luck. His son was the only young man left alive in the village. But Sei Weng kept his same attitude: despite all the turmoil, gains, and losses, he gave the same reply, "That's the way it is."

As William Shakespeare explained, "Nothing is either good or bad but thinking makes it so."

Victims give up their power by assuming that the world is to blame for their bad feelings and misfortune. They place the source of their problems "out there." But in doing so, they place their solutions in the same place – "out there" beyond their grasp.

How Victims See the World

How Owners See the World

Before they get to be happy, Victims have to fix the world and make people behave the way they want them to. This is exhausting and unfulfilling (not to mention impossible), so Victims tend to be frustrated and unhappy.

Where Victims see the world through the lens of "I'm upset because…", Owners claim their power by recognizing that their thinking is the source of their feelings. Specifically, they understand that their expectations and judgments create their negative emotions. Thus, they open to the possibility of creating happiness, independent of their circumstances.

Our negative emotions aren't caused by what happens to us, but by our judgments *about* what happens to us.

Instead of clinging to their thoughts and claiming that they're *true*, Owners engage in an ongoing inquiry about whether or not their thoughts are *useful*. They don't automatically believe every thought that runs through their mind. And they make a practice of noticing when they feel scared, sad, upset, or insecure, and use this as an opportunity to tune in to the voice of fear.

Whenever you're feeling upset or insecure, see if you've just stepped into playing the Victim. Do you believe that something "out there" is the cause of your negative feelings? Only the voice of fear would frame it that way. Instead of taking your thoughts and feelings at face value, pause. Reclaim your power. Make Friends with Your Fears. Question Deeply.

What is a relationship or situation that's upsetting you in some way? What's your "because"? (As in "I'm upset because...") In this situation, to what level are you being an Owner or a Victim?

Once you've taken ownership, the next step is to practice acceptance. In other words, to Make Friends with Your Fears. Instead of trying to fight your fears, get curious. If a belief is causing you pain, it's because you're scared to let it go. There's some reason why your fear has you holding on to it.

What is the fear? Why is it so important that you hold on to this judgment? What are you afraid might happen if your beliefs were wrong about a certain situation?

Let's look at one of my judgments: "If I'm going to be successful, I need to work all the time." When I tune in to my voice of fear, it says that it's scared about two different things: laziness and intimacy. My fears claim that if I let go of this belief, I'd stop pushing, get lazy, run out of motivation, and fail. Furthermore, I'd have nothing in place to pull me away from my family, so I'd get even closer and run a greater risk of being hurt. I could fly too close to the sun and get burned. Here, the voice of fear is trying to serve me the best way it knows how by keeping me motivated so I'll be successful and safe.

I never make it my goal to get rid of painful beliefs. My goal is to let go of the places where my fears feel the need to be right about these beliefs. Once I let go of my attachment to my beliefs, then I can get back to a clean and clear place of evaluation, where my beliefs serve me instead of running the show.

After ownership and acceptance, the third step is inquiry. Get curious. Is this thing you believe in even true? How do you know that it's true? Is it a fact or an opinion? Can you absolutely know for sure that it's true? What does it feel like when you believe this thought? What would it feel like if you didn't? What are the consequences of believing this thought? What would change if you didn't?

Questioning Deeply isn't a concept or an idea. It's a discipline, like learning to play the piano. It's an area of competence requiring systems, practices, and skills.

Byron Katie offers the best method of inquiry I've encountered. If you visit http://www.TheWork.com, you'll find a wide range of resources, many of them free, for developing one particular practice of Questioning Deeply.

Questioning Deeply is a master competency, one of the most valuable capacities you can develop. In all that you undertake – certainly any Leap of Faith – it will serve you to make Big Decisions and create Big Wins.

The next step in the process starts when you embrace the truth that Commitment Creates Value.

Chapter 36

Commitment Creates Value

"The quality of a person's life is in direct proportion to their commitment to excellence, regardless of their chosen field of endeavor." ~ Vince Lombardi

As an executive coach, I'm in the business of change. I help people get clear about what they most want, and then I help them create it in much more efficient ways than they could do on their own. Instead of providing information, I help people create transformation. It's what I get paid for.

Yet I've also learned that by themselves, my skills aren't really all that valuable.

I used to think that my tools were special, that I had the power to change lives. It sounded great and it made me feel important, until I discovered that the things I *do* create may be 10 percent of the value that my clients receive. Who I'm *being* – my current level on the ladder of consciousness – is much more important, but even that constitutes only about 30 percent of the value.

The most important ingredient by far is the level of commitment my clients bring to the table. It accounts for at least 60 percent of their results. When I'm working with people who are totally committed to transforming their lives, I could almost read the phone book to them and they'd find a way of creating value. But when someone is deeply committed to keeping change at bay, there's nothing I can do to help them.

Commitment creates value.

Now, it's easy to declare commitment. Heck, anyone can make a New Year's resolution, and they may even believe it. "I'm done with chocolate. That's it! I'm committed."

Yet most resolutions fail.

The problem is that most people think commitment is about willpower. It's not. A strong, successful commitment requires much more than just willpower.

It requires investment.

If you want to measure your true commitment to a goal, measure how much time, money, and energy you have been consciously and consistently putting behind it.

If you want to lose weight – great! How many hours a week have you scheduled on your calendar to work on this goal? How much money have you budgeted for healthier foods, a gym membership, and a personal trainer? And which of your current priorities have you decided to say no to as a way of freeing up the energy needed to make this change?

My parents, David and Zina, are two of the most loving people I know. They recently celebrated their 40th wedding anniversary, still love each other dearly, and provide one of my greatest role models for what a loving long-term marriage looks like. With a beautiful home overlooking the mountains, meaningful occupations, a deep religious and spiritual life, a large and loving community, four wonderful children, and a large flock of adorable grandchildren, they're living the American Dream. But when we've asked

COMMITMENT CREATES VALUE

them how they met and got married, they've regularly admonished us to make sure that – no matter what – we don't do things like they did.

My father was 27 when my birth mother suddenly died. One day he was a struggling but happy graduate student at Cornell, married to his college sweetheart, and the father of two beautiful young children. By the next day, his world had fallen apart. What had been a series of pleasant challenges for two young parents suddenly felt like an insurmountable mountain for one. In his anger, fear, self-judgment and grief, for a while he barely knew which way was up. Yet he had an unshakeable commitment to his children and their well being.

In what my father has described as one of the hardest and saddest days of his life, he bundled up his two little children; put us in the arms of our grandmother; and waved goodbye as we boarded a plane to Mexico City, where my sister and I were raised for six months in the mission home his parents were running there.

What comes next is one of the greatest examples of commitment I've experienced in my life. Fueled by his commitment to provide and care for his children, my father pulled himself together, got a new job as an assistant professor at the University of Illinois, bought a home there, flew out to Utah for a blind date with a woman named Zina, and by the end of a very intense and prayer-filled week with this new lady, had an engagement ring on her finger. He then flew back to New York, finished his Ph.D., and flew back to Utah for his second date with our new mother – their wedding.

Their honeymoon consisted of driving across the plains in a yellow Ryder van, stopping every few hours for gas, on their journey to a new home, in a new state, with a new job, and a new family. Our new mother never

199

even had the chance to meet her two new children until two months after their marriage. Many years later, after three decades of providing their four children with the most loving upbringing we could ask for, they explained to us just how challenging their first couple years of marriage were. But they made it work, buoyed by their commitment, their strong beliefs about marriage, the love and support of their family and church, and of course, my mother's dowry – a side of beef, cradled in dry ice, and carried in the back of a nervously happy moving van, to its new home in the Midwest.

Above all else, their story demonstrates a great truth.

Commitment creates value.

In creating deep change, the first key is to find your *Yes Yes Hell No!* In my parents' case, it was very clear – they had a deep spiritual knowing that their relationship was on course and inspired. They clearly knew that having two parents to raise the children was extremely important, and that they had a deep foundation of shared values upon which to draw. And there was no shortage of fear to complete the picture.

Then the second key is to Make Friends With Your Fears, which they did through faith and prayer. And the third key is commitment – to fully invest yourself in your decisions. Now, normally I wouldn't recommend committing yourself on the second date – but in this case it absolutely worked for them and for their deeply grateful children.

Often times the most valuable work I do with my coaching clients occurs *before* they sign up to work with me. It happens during the enrollment conversation, where we get clear on the heartfelt, specific, scary goals they most want to take on – and the size of the coaching fee that would truly commit them to doing so. Then when they commit to our relationship and pay that fee, they're engaging their goals in such a powerful way that the coaching itself tends to be straightforward.

William was a senior engineering manager who kept getting invited to interview for executive level positions. At three different companies, over the course of six years, he was given this opportunity, then fell apart in the interview, wasn't offered the promotion, and quit in a huff. After moving his family around the world three times as a result of his outbursts, his wife laid down the law. She explained that while she loved William and didn't want to get divorced, he either needed to get help in addressing his issues, or else things were headed that way.

In our initial conversations, we slowed things down and helped Jonathon take a different level of ownership for the choices he'd been making. We supported him in getting clear on the changes he most wanted to make, and the core patterns that had been holding him back.

At the time, my minimum coaching fee was $20,000 for six months – up front, in advance, and with no refunds. It took us about a month to get to the place where he was ready to make this level of commitment. It wasn't easy. His goals showed up as a huge *Yes, Yes, Hell No!* And the idea of making this level of investment in himself was a big Leap of Faith as well. Yet when he wrote that first check for $20,000 and mailed it to me, his life changed.

During our work together, the coaching felt almost embarrassingly easy. It was like I'd throw out a few seeds each call and by the next week he'd have turned them into a forest. William dove into his issues. He learned cutting edge tools for emotional mastery, conflict resolution, and authentic leadership. He embraced his fears and created deep change. In doing so, he became a star at work, turned his marriage around, and a year later called me up to let me know that he and his family had just had their best Christmas ever.

All because of how Commitment Creates Value.

Once you have a heartfelt, specific, and scary goal, ask yourself these four questions:

How many hours a week are you willing to commit to this goal? For how long?

How much money are you willing to invest in creating this result?

How much money would you need to invest to truly be committed to this goal?

What are you willing to say no to or let go of that would free up enough energy to create this change?

Did you do so? Congratulations! You've created a real commitment – something that has a great chance at succeeding. Now your job is to follow through on these investments.

And the single most powerful way to make sure you do so is to Receive Support.

Chapter 37

Receive Support

"Don't be shy about asking for help. It doesn't mean you're weak, it only means you're wise." ~ Anonymous

Imagine that you've just had a heart attack. Your heart stops beating and you fall to the floor. Someone calls for an ambulance while someone else administers CPR. Arriving quickly, the paramedics restart your heart. They rush you to the hospital where the doctors receive you instantly in the ER, only to decide that you need emergency surgery. They put your body on a heart and lung machine, rush you into the operating room, administer anesthesia, and crack your chest open with a rib spreader.

When you wake up – and thankfully, you do – the doctors explain that you've just had a triple heart bypass. They tell you that after you leave the hospital you'll have to make some serious changes in what you eat and how you exercise. If you don't, you'll likely have another heart attack within the next year or two.

The doctors, with their decades of experience, offer a literal ultimatum: change or die.

Would you change? Do you think you could? If so, how long do you think it would last?

Most people think they would change. After all, your life is on the line! But in reality, most don't.

In his book *Change or Die*, Alan Deutschman examines the lives of patients who were faced with exactly this dilemma: as part of their recovery from heart surgery, they *had* to make a change.

The results were shocking. While almost everyone made at least some moderate efforts for a few months, after two years, 90 percent of the patients had failed to change their lifestyle.

And many of them died shortly thereafter.

Please, don't stop reading. It gets better. Alan also demonstrated that with one particular group, 77 percent of the patients managed to make the necessary changes. 77 percent! Compared to 10 percent!

What was so special about this group? They weren't more successful, more motivated, or more intelligent. The difference had nothing to do with wealth, character, or education.

The difference was that they received support. Instead of imagining they should be able to make these changes on their own, they got help. And not just any help. They invested their time, money, and energy into a group coaching program that focused on what Alan calls the 3 R's: Reframe, Relate, and Repeat.

Their support started with a Reframe. Instead of focusing on the fear of dying, the group started by creating a new vision based on their joy of living. They picked a positive paradigm, connected with their highest priorities, and received help in integrating different habits into their daily lives. Change became more than just a "nice idea."

Then the next piece – Relate – involved being part of a support system that allowed them to build real relationships with other people who were dealing with the same experience. Instead of trying to create change on their own, they received support from the group and from their coach, and they got to give support as well.

The third key to creating sustained change was to Repeat the process. Instead of treating this as a short-term project, they committed to receiving support for an extended period of time.

There's a common truism in self-help: "It takes 30 days to make or break a habit." It's a great saying. Except that it's seldom true.

In this case, it took 12 to 18 months of consistent commitment. The patients who succeeded – and lived – were the ones who continued to invest in support until the changes were no longer something they "did" – they had become an automatic part of who they were and how they lived.

There are many ways you can Receive Support. Coaching is one way. So is counseling, being part of a 12-step program, joining a mastermind group, or working with an accountability partner.

The key is to make sure you're creating, committing to, and investing in a support structure that's bigger than your fears.

I know that this concept is foreign to many people, particularly in our independence-based culture. We're trained to think we should be able to do everything on our own. I certainly was. Yet growth is a team sport. While no one can do your growth work for you, it's also remarkably difficult to do it on your own.

But with the right support – including structures that meet the "3 R's" – growth shifts from being difficult to being fun.

Chapter 38

Pay It Forward

"You cannot out give the universe."~ Michael Beckwith

As you learn to leap, life gets better and better. As you receive support, life gets easier. And as you master the art of making wise decisions, life brims over with gifts.

From this place, your opportunity is to keep the cycle flowing. Give to others. Be of service. Make a difference.

Pay it forward.

Not because you should be generous, but because you want to be. Because it's one of the wisest choices you can make. Because giving from our overflow feels so good. And because service moves us up the ladder of consciousness – fast.

How do you create more love? You give it away. The same holds true for abundance. It's all about being part of a cycle of both giving and receiving.

There are many ways you can be of service. You can donate to a cause you care about. You can reach out a hand to someone in need. You can volunteer with a charity. Or you can take the time to truly listen to someone you love.

What are your gifts? What is your calling? How are you best able to contribute to the lives of others? For some people, it's through teaching or coaching. For others, it's through philanthropy, the arts, or public service. You can make a difference anywhere and anytime – at work, at home, through your church, in your community, wherever you feel called to reach out.

However you give, wherever you give, get greedy with your giving. Make a difference. It's a blast.

Here's an easy, powerful way to put service into practice.

Do you wish you'd learned these tools years ago? Can you imagine some of the mistakes you might have avoided, or the wins you might have created?

If so, I have two requests of you. First, please use this book. Don't just think about it. Put it into action. This isn't just a pile of ideas. It's a technology for transformation. Take advantage of it. Please! And if you're willing, I'd love for you to send me an email and tell me your story. What was the value you created by putting these tools into action? What was your *Yes Yes Hell No!?* How did your decision to follow it improve your life?

My second request is for you to Pay It Forward. If this book made an impact on you, please give a copy of it to ten people you care about. Besides being of service to them, this is also a way of creating support for yourself.

With the people you give it to, follow up and see how the book resonated for them. Ask them what they learned. And then ask them if they'd like to partner up with you, so you could help one another put these tools into practice. Create a team that you can share support with as a way of changing their lives, and as a way of changing your own.

On the website (*www.YesYesHellNo.com*) there are some structures and resources for how you can best support one another, as well as a special offer for how you can give these books away in a particularly meaningful and cost-effective way.

Thank you!

Make Your Life Your Masterpiece

"An old story tells of three stonecutters who were asked what they were doing. The first replied, 'I am making a living.' The second kept on hammering while he said, 'I am doing the best job of stonecutting in the entire country.' The third one looked up with a visionary gleam in his eyes and said, 'I am building a cathedral.'"
~ La Sagrada Familia, Barcelona

What is your purpose? Why are you here? What's the meaning of your life? In our world, many people never even stop to ponder these questions. They just get too busy trying to make it through each day. Until one day they're on their deathbed wondering what happened. "Where did my life go?" "What did I achieve?" "Was it all worthwhile?"

Other people obsess about these questions, searching high and low for just the right truths.

And a few people get busy creating their own answers, one day at a time.

The meaning of life comes from growth, contribution, connection, and creativity. It comes from raising your level of consciousness and helping others do the same.

That's why we're here. It's your purpose and it's mine.

It's what we all have in common. It's what binds us together. Underneath all the stress and scarcity, it's what we agree on, because it's who we truly are.

You are love itself, when you are not afraid.

The *purpose* of life comes from these simple shared ingredients and others like them such as joy, laughter, love, and compassion.

The *beauty* of life comes from the virtually limitless ways you can mix these elements together. How do you choose to grow? Who do you choose to build your life with? What causes do you choose to focus on? Which tools and support structures do you choose to invest in? And with each action you take, what motivation do you draw on to move forward?

Your unique answers create your unique journey, and your journey is important. Not just to yourself, but also to the world.

Your life matters. There is no one like you. There never has been and there never will be. Your life is a precious work of art. You've been given a canvas and a big set of paints. You've been given teachers, role models, friends, and family. There's a whole party of people here to cheer you on.

How will you use this opportunity? What picture will you paint?

Here is my challenge and my invitation to you.

Make your life your masterpiece.

You have the opportunity to create a meaningful, happy, purpose filled life. Do so. Live fully. Embrace everything. Have fun. Make a difference. Love with all your heart. Live the life you were meant to live. Create a work of art.

One Leap of Faith at a time.

Next Steps

The *Yes Yes Hell No!* tool can be used to create breakthrough results in a range of different areas.

If you want to **transform your leadership** and learn how to use this tool to resolve conflicts, develop culture, build amazing teams, and motivate others to create deep change, please visit:

www.CoreCoaching.org

For examples of how to use this tool to **create extraordinary relationships**, including how to pick a great partner and how to develop greater intimacy in the face of your fears, please visit:

www.YesYesHellNo.com

If you are a coach, counselor, healer or other type of purpose driven service professional, and would like to learn how to use this tool to **enroll high paying clients in ways that you absolutely love**, please visit:

www.SellingByGiving.com

To **join the *Yes Yes Hell No!* community**, where you can share stories about Leaps of Faith you have taken, and the results you've created by applying this tool in different areas of your life, please visit:

www.YesYesHellNo.com

And if you are interested in **mastering this tool in a live setting**, where you will find and commit to your Big Wins, learn how to make Big Decisions, and Make Friends With Your Fears, please visit:

www.BigWinWeekend.com

Acknowledgements

To my wife, Nicole. Thank you for being the love of my life.

To my daughters, Annibelle and Leilanna. Thank you for challenging me each day to expand my heart and receive even more of your love.

To my parents, David, Renee and Zina. Thank you for teaching me the ultimate value of family, and how to love with all my heart.

To my brother and sisters, Shauna, Brad and Katie. Thank you for all the love and laughter, and for loving me just the way I am.

To my teachers, Ron and Mary Hulnick. Thank you holding space for my healing, transformation, and growth. You do miraculous work.

To my coach, Steve Chandler. Thank you for showing me just what the path of master coaching can be.

To my friend, Jeff Shaw. Thank you for giving me the push I needed to sit down and write this book.

To my mentor, Jack Canfield. Thank you for modeling what it means to be such a master student, teacher, and transformational leader.

To my investors, colleagues, and friends at GlobalCast and Talarian. Thank you trusting me, even when I had no idea what I was doing.

To my editor, Jayalalita. Thank you for helping this book take form and become what it was meant to be.

To Christine Kloser, Marlene Oulton, Ranilo Cabo, and

Carrie Jareed. Thank you for turning my manuscript into this beautiful published book.

To Kelly, Chelsea and Nicholas. Thank you for being the team that I trust, for the lives you touch, and for the amazing work that you do.

To my clients. Thank you for letting me serve you and for helping me develop my own learning and leadership.

B y the age of 30, Brian had earned a Berkeley Ph.D. in computer science, raised $20 million for two Silicon Valley startups, become an internationally known academic and speaker, been part of a $400 million IPO, repeatedly made and lost millions – and burned out twice. After an emotional crisis, he left his career for six years of full-time personal growth work, including a M.A. in Spiritual Psychology from the University of Santa Monica.

Today, Brian serves as an executive coach, leadership consultant, and keynote speaker. He helps leaders turn soft skills into hard results, and supports them in developing companies that both make money and make a difference. He is considered one of the foremost experts in the fields of conscious business and authentic leadership.

That said, what *really* excites Brian is his family. He lives in Los Angeles with his wife Nicole, where they spend much of their time wondering how their two daughters can be so cute.

Made in USA - North Chelmsford, MA
1161699_9780986309007
09.09.2020 1327